THE LOMBARDO STORY

The Lombardo Story

BEVERLY FINK CLINE

Musson Book Company
a division of General Publishing Co. Limited
Don Mills, Ontario

Published 1979 by
Musson Book Company
a division of
General Publishing Co. Limited
30 Lesmill Road
Don Mills, Ontario. M3B 2T6

First Printing

Canadian Cataloguing in Publication Data

Cline, Beverly Fink, 1951-
  The Lombardo Story

Includes index.
ISBN 0-7737-0042-0

1. Lombardo, Guy, 1902-1977. 2. Lombardo family.
3. Musicians—Biography. 4. Royal Canadians (Dance band)
  I. Title

ML422.L76C56   785′.092′4   C79-094403-0

Design by Maher and Murtagh

Printed and bound in Canada

For Leigh—husband, friend, and musician

Contents

Preface

★ ★ ★ ★ ★ ★ ★ ★ ★ ★ ★ ★

Over sixty years ago, three brothers from London, Ontario, Gaetano (Guy), Carmen, and Lebert Lombardo, formed a band which they named the Lombardo Brothers Concert Company. Starting in 1914 and accompanied by their father's rich baritone voice, their sister Elaine's dancing, and their friend Freddie Kreitzer's nimble fingers on piano, they toured London and the surrounding countryside. They played for church parties, garden clubs, coming-out parties, and the occasional dance. From this humble beginning, the brothers, by a combination of talent, ambition, hard work, and some sheer old-fashioned good luck, became the leaders of North America's best-known and best-respected dance band, Guy Lombardo and the Royal Canadians.

This book tells in words and pictures the story of the meteoric rise of the band and the family that made it possible.

While I was growing up in London I often heard tales of the "Lombardo boys," as they are affectionately known in our hometown. The Lombardos and my family have been friends since the early years of this century. The Lombardo boys used to buy their penny candy from my great-grandfather's general store, and my grandfather used to be a fill-in pianist with the band when Freddie wanted a night off and they were still in London.

Not only is this book the Lombardo story, it is a tribute to the Lombardo brothers, the three men who brought popular music into the living rooms of all America. Unfortunately, only Lebert is alive now to read this tribute; Carmen died in 1971 and Guy in 1977. However, the Lombardo tradition is still strong, continuing, and vital, for Bill Lombardo, Lebert's son, is the new bandleader of the Royal Canadians.

The Royal Canadians' sound now, as always, is relaxed, danceable, lively, and easy to dream along with. "Remember the time we . . ." the music seems to say.

Lebert, Bill, Elaine (Lombardo), and Kenny Gardner, the band's vocalist for thirty-four years, have helped with this book, providing stories and pictures never printed before. The Lombardo family feels that this book needs to be written. As Kenny Gardner says, "The truth of the Lombardo family is just as charming, just as unique, and just as sincere as the myth."

This book is a relaxed look at the Lombardo music and personalities, the Royal Canadians' past, present, and future. There is so much to enjoy in the story of the men and women who made possible "the sweetest music this side of heaven."

Beverly Fink Cline
Toronto 1978

Acknowledgments

There are always so many people to thank when writing a book. I apologize in advance for anyone I've inadvertently left out.

I want to thank my husband, Leigh Cline, for suggesting that I write this book. Without his prodding and encouragement not only would it never have been begun, it certainly never would have been finished. As a musician he was able to help me greatly.

Nor could it have been written without the friendly and generous assistance of the Lombardo family, in particular Mr. Lebert Lombardo, Mr. and Mrs. Kenny Gardner, and Mr. Bill Lombardo. Thanks also to Gina Lombardo, for her help with pictures, and to Mr. and Mrs. Hubert Lombardo for their interview and help in contacting family members. To the Lombardo family, a great vote of thanks!

Thanks also to Royal Canadian band members Mr. Freddie Kreitzer, Mr. George Gowans, and Mr. Bernard Davies.

Thanks also to Mr. Alec Davidson who spent many hours reading the manuscript and providing information and pictures.

Miss Ruth Andres, Mr. Dewey Bergman, Mr. Don Byrnes, and the late Saul Richman all graciously helped by sharing their Lombardo moments with me.

Mr. Dave Kressley kindly allowed me to use his research about the Lombardos, particularly his work on Carmen Lombardo. Many thanks to Dave and his fellow researcher, Mr. Dick Scher.

In particular, thanks to my agent and friend, Lucinda Vardey, who looks after everything so well and leaves me free to write.

Thanks to my editor at General Publishing, Julie Beddoes, for her friendly and helpful suggestions. To all the others at General Publishing who put in time working on this book, thank you!

My London, Ontario relatives, namely my parents Mr. and Mrs. A. Fink, my grandparents Mr. and Mrs. W. Weinstein and Mrs. Bessie Fink, and my great-aunt Mrs. Lillian Kroll, all deserve tons of thanks for the queries they answered, and in the case of my parents, the personal introductions they made for me.

Thanks to my special friend, Dr. Clara Thomas, who is always ready to help and be there when I need her.

The following people also helped in putting this book together and I'd like to express my gratitude to them: A. A. Linnell, Dr. J. Babatzannis, Mr. Jamie Bell, Mr. Norman Bradford, Mr. Bill Brady, Mr. Mark Breslin, Mr. Leonard Cofield, Mrs. M. A. (Campbell) Drummond, Ms. Moira Egan, Mr. and Mrs. Sam Frank, Ms. Sue Fink, Mr. and Mrs. A. Frank, Mr. Elwood Glover, Ms. Beryl Greenspan, Mr. Omar F. Haselgrove, Mrs. B. Herbert, Mr. W. D. Lamont, Ms. Joanne Le Vine, Mrs. Cora Matthews, Mr. J. E. O'Doud, Mr. Jim Simpson, Mrs. C. B. Sleth, Mr. Bill Smith (of Jazz and Blues Record Store, Toronto), Mr. Vic Waring, Mrs. O. H. (Barbara) Warwick, Dr. D. C. Williams, Ms. Cathy Van Baren, Variety Magazine, and Mr. Selby Young.

This book was written with the generous assistance of the Ontario Arts Council.

B.F.C.

Introduction

Dear Friends,

Reading this book has brought back so many memories of my years so far as a Royal Canadian. Looking back on the beginnings of the band, it seems incredible that my brothers and I, four boys from London, Ontario, could get so far in the music business. But we did and it's been great! We've had such exciting moments and met such great people. Through all our travels so many kind people have come to hear us and dance to our music.

My brothers and I were blessed enough to all be in the same band. Mama and Papa saw to that as they saw to so many other things. We only hope that through our music we were able to give them back some of the love and happiness they gave to us.

The years have been good to me. I'm still a Royal Canadian and I love playing night after night and meeting our fans. My son, Bill, is now our bandleader, and it makes me very proud to see him out there in front. He understands our music and knows what a privilege it is to be a Royal Canadian. We go onstage every night with the same objective that Guy, Carmen, Victor, and I have always had . . . we just want to play good music and make our fans happy.

I think you will like this book. I know I did!

Lebert Lombardo

"The truth of the Lombardo family is just as charming, just as unique, and just as sincere as the myth."

Kenny Gardner

1
How It All Began

Mama Lombardo, born Angelina Paladino, was the first Italian child born in London, Ontario, and she passed to her sons and daughters a great pride in being Londoners and Canadians.

Mama's parents had arrived in London in the early 1880s. En route from the Aeolian island of Lipari to Buenos Aires, a violent storm forced the passengers of their ship to disembark on Ellis Island, New York, and Carmelo Paladino, his young wife, and their baby daughter Mary found themselves on American soil. Carmelo read an advertisement in an Italian New York newspaper that would take him and his family to a country he had never heard of.

It seems an Italian engineer named Count Rhubingino was searching for oil in Petrolia near London, Ontario and was looking for a tailor to work for him. Carmelo, who was a tailor and who was young and adventurous, answered the advertisement, was accepted, and went to set up shop in London.

Carmelo's business prospered and he soon found he needed apprentices. Being family-minded, Paladino wrote his distant cousins the Lombardos, who also lived on Lipari, suggesting that the Lombardo sons come to Canada.

The Lombardos' homeland island of Lipari, part of a volcanic group just north of Sicily, has been known for centuries as a leading exporter of pumice and a major producer of dyes. The Lombardos, descendants of the ancient Germanic tribe, the Lombards, which immigrated to Italy around 586 AD and founded a kingdom which reached its height during the seventh and eighth centuries, have a history of hard work and diligence that pays off in success.

Elaine Lombardo Gardner, Guy's sister, tells of her grandparents' dyeworks business which was so successful the family could afford a summer home: "My dad told us that his mother always said that she never saw her husband's arms when they weren't blue. Navy blue was the only color they made. They had a summer home which they called the *mutto* which means 'the mountain' in Italian. It was way up high. My grandfather could never go there because he had to keep the fires going to keep the dye at the right temperature. When the rest of the family went up there for the summer, every night at about eight my grandmother would take a lantern and wave it to and fro so my grandfather could see from the dyeworks that everything was all right."

Grandfather's industrious, ambitious sons, Vincent, Fred, and Frank Lombardo, eager to avoid the military draft in Lipari, set off for London in answer to the summons. Only Gaetano Lombardo, the youngest son, remained on the island. Gaetano's father was happy that his three eldest sons prospered in Canada and liked Canadian life; however, he wanted Gaetano to remain in Italy and continue the family business. But Gaetano was restless and unhappy with his father's plans for him. Gaetano quite simply loved music and was blessed with a good ear and a rich baritone voice. Opportunities for musical instruction and performance were limited on tiny Lipari, and Gaetano wanted desperately to come to Canada, be a tailor, and make enough money to study music. His father relented. In 1887, aged fourteen, Gaetano arrived in London, speaking no English and wearing a name tag pinned to his chest.

Gaetano thrived in London. By the age of twenty-eight he had set up his own tailoring establishment on London's main avenue, Dundas Street. He worked long and hard hours, but also found time to continue his education, take voice lessons, and add his baritone voice to the YMCA choir.

By 1900 it became clear that Angelina, Carmelo's second daughter, and Gaetano had fallen in love and wished to marry. Angelina's mother was opposed to the match because the eldest daughter, Mary, was as yet unwed. Angelina was firm in her resolve, but Mrs. Paladino was unmoved. Angelina had already broken tradition by adopting a career. Angelina had five sisters and she was the only one who went out to work. In the late 1890s Italian girls stayed at home until they married. Angelina went to business college, learned to type and take shorthand, and landed herself a

Angelina and Gaetano Lombardo with their famous family.

plum job as secretary to a Mr. Cronyn of the influential banking
and lawyer family. (Mr. Cronyn, incidentally, was the grandfather
of actor Hume Cronyn.) Now she wished to break tradition again
by marrying before Mary. Gaetano didn't care that Angelina could
neither cook nor sew, and he didn't love Mary. So in 1901 the
Paladinos relented. The couple were married and they settled into a
little cottage on London's Oxford Street.

In 1902 Gaetano Jr. (Guy) was born, not in the little cottage his
father and mother had moved into when they married, but in an
airy brick house. It was a move upward for the quick-minded Papa
Lombardo. The Lombardo family grew quickly. Carmen was born
in 1903, and Lebert in 1905. The three musical brothers, so close in
age, would always be close in spirit; nothing would ever come between them. Elaine, the first daughter, was born soon after Lebert,
followed by brothers Joseph and Victor. Rosemarie, the baby of the
family, in fact the darling, was born much later in 1925.

The city of London was incorporated in 1854; in the early 1900s it retained the atmosphere of a small town. The Lombardo brothers enjoyed this atmosphere. Everyone knew everyone else it seemed and, as the boys wandered home from school, cookies and milk were freely dispensed to them by neighbors and relatives.

Papa and Mama Lombardo were Roman Catholic in belief and spirit. However, during the early years of their childhood, the Lombardo children did not go to St. Peter's, the Catholic school, but to the local public school on Simcoe Street. The basis for the Lombardos' decision was logistical. St. Peter's was over two miles away and over rail tracks from their home; Mama felt her children were too young to venture this long distance by themselves. Simcoe Street School was simply around the corner. Lebert and Elaine remember the parish priest coming to the house to inquire when the Lombardo children would change schools. By the time Guy was nine, the change was made, and he was in charge of making sure his brothers and Elaine reached school and home safely.

When Guy was nine and Carmen eight, their musical education was begun. Papa had promised himself way back on Lipari that his children would be afforded the opportunity to study music. The tailor shop on Dundas Street was set up as musical headquarters for the boys. It was a booming place, with eleven tailors working under Mr. Lombardo's guidance. Papa had cleverly secured the commission to produce all the white jackets for the University of Western Ontario's Medical School.

A three-quarter sized violin was given to Guy and a flute to Carmen. Carmen later changed to the saxophone, an instrument on which he was to become world famous as a leader in tone and style. Soon after, Lebert, slightly younger than his brothers, was introduced to the harp. This acquaintance lasted only a short time; Lebert had profoundly different ideas. He had already started to show in what direction his musical talents and interests lay. Lebert had acquired an old army bugle and delighted in screeching out notes. A broken tooth from a hockey game squelched the early stages of his association with the trumpet. The bugle was stuck on the branch of a tree where Lebert used it as practice for his BB gun. Lebert turned his attention in another direction. He pulled out the spindles from Mama's kitchen chairs and tapped on the table, the window glass, the sills. Finally Papa bought Lebert a set of drums.

Papa and Mama set up a tough and vigorous regimen for the boys that would last for about the next five years. Guy and Carmen were expected to be at Papa's tailor shop at eight in the morning to practice their music, then to go off to school. After school the boys

GUY LOMBARDO

Courtesy of Alec David

A rare picture of Guy playing his violin.

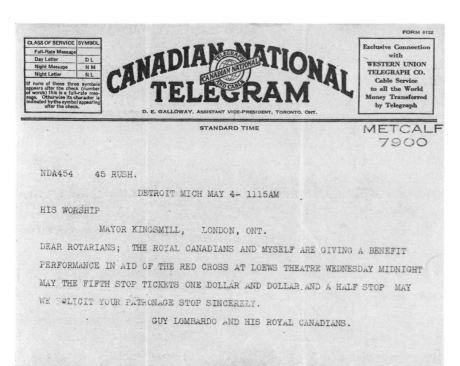

Courtesy of Mrs. Cora Matthews

The Lombardo brothers kept alive their connections with their hometown as this telegram, sent in 1937, demonstrates.

returned to the shop and practiced a further two hours before they accompanied Papa home for dinner. For any young boy this would be a demanding routine, but for the athletic, vigorous, and adventurous Guy and Carmen, it was particularly hard. There was just too much to explore, too many games to play, too many people to meet. Simcoe Street was a lively little community, distinguished by large, airy homes and a boisterous immigrant population. Many of the people in the neighborhood spoke languages other than English, and the variety of languages, customs, and foods gave a sparkle to the area. Incidentally, Papa and Mama Lombardo seldom spoke Italian around the home because they wanted the children to speak English well, with good grammar. Later in life Guy would have cause to wish he could speak the language when Italian well-wishers greeted him warmly in the tongue.

Papa was a strict disciplinarian, not averse to using the cane if needed. The boys complied with Papa's schedule, and he rewarded them with time for enjoying the neighborhood's delights. Omar Haselgrove, a neighbor, remembers with amusement the limitations on Guy's and Carmen's free time. "After four o'clock and on Saturdays," he says, "we could all play ball on what was then known as Carling Flats, at the back of the Carling brewery along the Thames River. Carmen and Guy would not play too long. We would see them going one way from the diamond and in the opposite direction would be Mr. Lombardo with his cane. They had to practice pretty steadily, but I guess in later years they thanked him."

The Lombardo boys loved the water, a love which led to Guy's later interest in speedboat racing. The old swimming hole of their childhood days was behind the present-day Labatt's Brewery and formed a part of the Thames River (named in the eighteenth century by the colony's English Lieutenant-Governor John Graves Simcoe). During a visit to London in 1950, Guy and Carmen went to see their childhood haunts. They visited the swimming hole and looked for the "clay rock" from which they used to dive. "That hill was tough; it was really tough and it used to be two jumps up," Guy said.

Another favorite stop for the Lombardo boys was McCormick's cookie factory, just across the street from Papa's tailor shop. A good practice meant a reward. For young boys, cookies, candy, and crackers were just the thing.

Papa provided more exhilarating amusements for the children. Even before he was married, Gaetano Lombardo Sr. had a horse and buggy. When the boys were growing up, Papa took to racing his trotting horses. It was a characteristic of both Papa and Guy that they liked speed, whether it was in horses, cars, or boats. Elaine remembers the horse races well: "All the men would race their horses every Sunday afternoon on Dufferin Avenue, right in front of St. Peter's Cathedral. That was a big, wide road and they would start right at the church and go up the street. Dad always loved horses and boats."

Papa also bought a houseboat. Elaine remembers, "When we were little kids, Mama just loved to stay home on Sunday with Joseph and Victor because they were younger. But Dad would take us, Guy, Carm, Lebe and me, down on the houseboat, and we would go by water to Springbank Park. One day we were all on the houseboat and Mama had made a basket lunch. There was a motor with a big rubber propeller, and Dad was doing something with a spark plug and it fell—and all of a sudden a flame! Luckily someone was coming down the opposite way and Papa knew him. All I can remember is my Dad picking us up and putting us over the side onto this oncoming boat. Dad stayed with the boat until the fire was out. The boat wasn't destroyed, but I guess Dad got a little panicky."

Kenny Gardner, vocalist with the band for thirty-eight years and Elaine's husband, describes his father-in-law's love of hobbies this way: "He had a very charming philosophy. In his last years his health became precarious and we wanted him and Mother to be close by in case they needed help. So Guy found them a little cottage on the south shore of Long Island, just about a block from his own house. There was a beautiful little speedboat out in front, right on the water. We'd go over there and he'd sidle up to me and say, 'Kenny, let's buy a boat.' And I'd say, 'Dad, how am I going to justify that? What am I going to use it for?' And he said, 'Listen, every man should have a hobby he can't afford.' "

Papa was never frivolous, however, and money for the children's music lessons was put aside before all else.

Papa believed that before you played piano or any instrument, you learned to read music. After that, you would have to learn the particular fingerings and styling of your instrument, but you would not be struggling to read every note. Therefore, each Lombardo child was sent to an Italian Londoner named Professor Vanuta, in order to study the Italian method of reading music, a method

Phyfe Photo

Elaine, Mama, and Rosemarie Lombardo.

The Lombardo Boys—Victor, Carmen, Lebert, and Guy—in the late 1960s.

named solfeggio. This, of course, was in addition to Guy's violin lessons, Carmen's flute lessons, and Lebert's harp and trumpet lessons. As well, each child began to study piano when he or she was eight years old! Papa even brought a piano teacher from Toronto to London each week!

Daughter Elaine was chosen to be the pianist of the family. Practice was not as rigidly controlled for her. Because the piano was too big to be moved into the tailor shop, Elaine practiced under Mama's less watchful eye. However, Elaine wanted to be a secretary like her mother and ultimately had her way.

In 1914, Guy and Carmen made their first public musical performance on a lawn behind a church. This appearance, however, almost did not take place, for Mama had an idea that delighted her and Papa and horrified twelve-year-old Guy and eleven-year-old Carmen. Elaine remembers the family argument vividly: "Mother told Dad that it would be nice if the boys had some kind of uniform when they played for the Mothers' Club: Lord Fauntleroy outfits—white collar, black silk tie, tight pants to just below the knees with buttons, black velveteen, a white blouse, little black jackets, and patent leather oxfords. Dad made them.

"The night they were to appear at the Mothers' Club, he brought the suits home. Guy and Carm said, 'We're not going to wear those! They're sissy! We're not going to wear them!' The house on Horton Street had a big square hall with four steps up to a landing and four steps down into the dining room. I can remember that night: Guy and Carm and Dad running around from the hall to the living room to the dining room, up the steps and down the steps, trying to put those velveteen suits on. Just then George Phillips, who lived down the street and was their friend, came into the house, and Papa must have told him he made those suits for them. Dad said, 'Try them on. Show George what they look like.' George's mother was a dressmaker. Well, he went head over heels over this uniform. He said he was going to get his mother to make him one. And that was the only reason they wore them!"

So began the musical Lombardos.

2 Friends, Fans, and Family

⭐ ⭐ ⭐ ⭐ ⭐ ⭐ ⭐ ⭐ ⭐ ⭐ ⭐ ⭐

Freddie Kreitzer lived close by the Lombardos in London, Ontario, and played with the band for over fifty years.

Encouraged by the enthusiastic reception of his two eldest sons' duets by the church groups around London, Papa formed the Lombardo Brothers Concert Company. First to be recruited was pianist Freddie Kreitzer, a young boy around Guy's age. Mrs. Lombardo and Mrs. Kreitzer knew each other, as Mrs. Lombardo was president of the Mothers' Club of Simcoe Street School, and Mrs. Kreitzer held the same position at South Public School. It has always been said that Mrs. Lombardo heard Freddie play the piano and decided that he would be an asset to Guy and Carmen. This is not entirely true. Freddie explains, "As far as joining the band, that was through my mother and Mrs. Lombardo. Only I wasn't playing the piano the night she heard me; I was playing a drum solo. I always played the piano, but for some reason I liked to play drum solos. I used to get someone to play some overture and I'd play the drums along with it. I didn't know how to play. I never took lessons on the drums." But Freddie had taken piano lessons for years and was already showing a versatility and style that was uniquely his.

Freddie's mother was born near the Plains of Abraham in Quebec, of English descent. His father was of German descent, and as this was during World War I, Freddie was given the nickname Enemy. The name stuck with Freddie for the more than fifty years that he was part of the Royal Canadians.

Lebert was recruited next, at nine years old, to be the drummer.

Elaine, at eight, danced, played the piano, and sang duets with Carmen, songs such as "The Girl Who Stuttered and the Boy Who Lisped." Papa would sing classical songs. Elaine wore the accordion-pleated dresses of the day, dresses made of yellow, pink, or white Chinese silk, beneath a little black velvet vest. The boys, Guy, Carmen, Lebert, and Freddie, wore business suits, the trousers being knickers.

Sometimes, as was fashionable then, an elecutionist was included in the company. She was from Detroit, a very pretty blue-eyed girl, who wore a blond curly wig in the Shirley Temple style and short bouffant skirts. She was supposed to be a doll that Elaine, playing the part of a young girl (as she really was) would wake up and delightedly see. The elecutionist would strut straight-limbed onto the stage and Elaine would dance her delight. Papa was the choreographer.

Papa bought a seven-passenger Studebaker in 1915, and Mama joined the entourage as they played strawberry socials and lawn parties all around the London area. Joseph and Victor, too young to participate, were safely left with Grandma Paladino back in London.

Alec Davidson, an old friend of the Lombardo brothers, says that

Courtesy of Freddie Kreitzer

The band at a recording session in 1924.

these neighborhood jaunts were responsible for one of the trademark sounds of the Royal Canadians. "When they were traveling with their father as a little concert group, they'd go as far as Jarvis, Ontario, sixty-five miles from London. In that area there were a lot of Scottish people and that's how the little bit of Scottish music got into their repertoire. They were conscious of their audience, and they had that little touch. You know, they do things like 'The Hop Scotch Polka.' "

It has also been said that the waltz rhythm, so typical of the Lombardo sound, stems from this period. Little Lebert would fall asleep over his drums and Papa would take over. The only rhythm that Papa knew was the waltz.

The Lombardo Brothers Concert Company received anywhere from nothing to about sixteen dollars for each of these jobs. As this was wartime, the family often drove to nearby hospitals, playing benefits for the returned soldiers.

At the end of World War I, the Lombardo boys displayed their early business sense. They had been selling Toronto newspapers in London on and off for some time. On Armistice Day, 1918, Guy heard that the *London Free Press* was going to publish a special Armistice edition at two o'clock that morning. The brothers and a school chum by the name of George McCullagh (who would later own the Toronto *Mail and Empire*), got as many copies of these papers as they could and rushed into the streets announcing the end of the war. Surprised Londoners dashed out to buy, and the four boys made a considerable sum of money!

By 1915 and 1916 the Concert Company was very busy, appearing often and playing songs such as "When You Wore a Tulip," "There's a Long Long Trail," and "Margie." Papa was getting worried. He had intended music to be a hobby for his children; now it seemed that it was becoming the most important thing in their lives. If they were to be musicians, Papa reasoned, they had better do it properly. Lebert relates: "We were missing a lot of school because in the early days you had to go to jobs in a horse and buggy. We'd get home late and we'd miss school. Dad said, 'It's interfering with your school.' So he stopped us for a while. If I'm not mistaken there was another time he stopped us. 'Well,' he said, 'if they want you they're going to have to pay you.' " Guy and Carmen both finished public school. Lebert says that he thinks he only went to the end of grade five as he was a few years younger.

Lebert's greatest memento of all his years as a musician is the first check the Lombardos ever received. This was from one of North America's greatest innovators and inventors, Sir Adam Beck, the

The first check ever received by the Lombardo band was signed by Sir Adam Beck, the Londoner in charge of the first generating station at Niagara Falls.

Canadian who harnessed Niagara Falls to produce electricity. The concert company played for Sir Adam's daughter's coming-out party. What a gala event that must have been! Dated 1918, the check drawn on Beck's London and Port Stanley Railroad Company, is for thirty-five dollars and seventy cents, a large sum of money for the sixteen-year-old Guy and his brothers.

How the check, endorsed so many years ago by Papa, made its way back to the Lombardo brothers is an interesting story in itself. According to Lebert, one of the professors at the University of Western Ontario in London had it up until a few years ago. When Guy returned to London to receive an honorary doctorate in music, the professor presented it to him as a gift. The Lombardos do not know how the check fell into the hands of the professor.

By 1919 the Lombardo boys had left school permanently and were professional musicians. The band now consisted of the boys, Freddie, a guitarist named Francis "Muff" Henry, and a trombonist by the name of Jeff Dillon. Carmen was teaching two London boys to play the sax, a beginning that would later result in the famous Lombardo sax section and trio.

During the winters the band played London and the surrounding countryside; during the summers the band played six nights a week at Springbank Park. The park, London's loveliest recreation and amusement area, is situated on the bank of the Thames River, a river much less polluted at that time. One of its greatest attractions was the sulphur-water drinking pump. Silly as that sounds, one drink from that cold, sparkling, vibrant pump was enough to make any skeptic a lifelong devotee. Unfortunately, it is now out of action.

The pavilion where the boys played was in the amusement section of the park. Listeners stood on a catwalk of the circular affair; the bandstand was above them and the floor below.

Mr. W. D. Lamont of London, a devoted fan of the Lombardos, tells the following story of meeting Guy at Springbank those many years ago: "I used to love to dance to their music. When I first met Guy, he was at Springbank Park, conducting his band at the old dancehall. It was located on what they called the American side near the roller coaster and games of chance, ice cream, soft drinks, shooting gallery, etc. The streetcars used to run from London to Springbank. At night the cars were always loaded with people. I think the price was five cents each way, not many cars in those days.

"Elaine was singing with Guy's orchestra and most of the players were her brothers too, but Guy was the leader of the band and what he said or did, that was it! I thought it would be nice if Elaine could get on the dance floor for maybe one dance. I got nerve enough to call Guy over to the edge of the platform. I asked him if it would be possible to have a dance with his good-looking sister Elaine. I'll never forget Guy's remark to me though it's fifty years ago more or less. 'Listen,' he said, 'we are getting *paid* to *play* and *sing*, but not to dance.' But with a smile on his face he said, 'Maybe we could arrange for you to have *one* dance with her, not *two* dances.' I thanked him and he went over and told his sister, who was a lovely dancer.

"So after that, any time I was there, I would put up one finger and Guy would point over to his sister. He would ask me, 'What would you like, a slow dance or something else?' I would say, 'You're the leader and whatever you say is OK with me if it suits Elaine.' I told her how I asked for a dance. I said, 'He probably thinks I've got a lot of nerve.' She said, 'Guy is a real brother, no better. He knows I like to dance with you. But I am going to tell you something. Guy wouldn't let me dance with you if you weren't dressed perfectly—shoes shined, hair combed, perfect white shirt, and bow tie.' He was very particular and his band was dressed just so. He said it gave a poor impression if they were not looking nice for the public to watch.

"So I thought I was lucky to be the only one that got to dance with Elaine while she was at his dances."

Guy and his band rented rehearsal space in London, and started putting together new arrangements that suited their sound. They bought the music of all the current favorites, such as Paul Whiteman and Isham Jones and traveled to Detroit to hear the likes

In the early days . . .

Courtesy of Alec Davidson

of Ted Fiorito, the Jean Goldkette group, and the Pasternak-Rubenstein band. Carmen joined the Pasternak-Rubenstein group in 1922, at nineteen, and made the sum of $125 a week. He returned to play with his brothers in 1923. From the Pasternak-Rubinstein group, Carmen learned a valuable lesson. Rather than play the typical "businessmen's bounce" jaunty rhythms, this Detroit band slowed down the tempo, making it easier to dance to. Carmen brought this idea home, an idea that was to develop into a Lombardo trademark.

Carmen was a virtuoso saxophonist. Omar Haselgrove remembers him this way: "When I was nineteen or twenty I belonged to the Forest City Club of London, which was on the corner of Dundas and Richmond. The Lombardos were members there as well as another orchestra that belonged to Jack McCormick. One Sunday the Lombardos had been practicing there and Carmen was kidding around with solos on his sax. He finally asked Jack McCormick to play a solo on his sax. But Jack replied, 'Not after you, Carmen. You're too good.' Carmen said, 'Tell me what you will play and I will finger it while you blow into it,' which they did, and you would have sworn it was Carmen all by himself up there."

In 1922 the Lombardo band was hired to play winters at a place called the Winter Garden in London. The Winter Garden was the "in" spot then to dance, and all the bands that had played there in previous winters had been from the United States. Freddie Kreitzer recalls, "We played around for a few years, and I left for a while and I was playing at Loews Theatre or the Allen. Guy got the job at Springbank, and I played with them for a while there and then once again at the theaters. I finally rejoined them at the Winter Garden and I never left them from then on."

In the winter of 1923 the band acquired another member, Londoner George Gowans. George had known the Lombardos for many years and was a friend. "I had played with Harold Skinner's band," he says, "and when they amalgamated both bands, Lebert was playing drums and I was playing xylophone. Then I went to drums.

"The one trumpet player that Guy had at the time at the old Winter Garden, well, they got into an argument and I guess he got fired. Lebert had been fooling around with the trumpet so Guy said to Lebert, 'You're the trumpet player,' and I happened to be at the Garden that night and he said, 'You're the drummer.' "

The band finished the winter of 1922 at the Winter Garden and won a coveted summer job playing at Port Stanley, a resort town near London. Port Stanley, on Lake Erie, was quiet, prestigious, and peaceful, and the band played in a pavilion down on the lake. The boys lived together in a cottage there. The author's grandfather, Wally Weinstein, who used to fill in occasionally for Freddie, remembers the cottage well and observes that the Port Stanley job, with the independence it allowed the boys in living away from home did much to mature the band members.

On June 19, 1923, Guy's birthday, an event occurred that would change the Lombardo brothers' outlook, expand their horizons, and send their heads whirling. Elaine tells the story: "In 1923 Isham Jones was very big. Well, he was to come to London in the summer of 1923. I think he was playing at the Winter Garden and the boys were playing at Port Stanley. They wanted to get home to London to hear Isham Jones. I forget what they did, something with the electric lights, or some other trick, so they could get time off to come to London.

"In the meantime, Mother and Dad were very friendly with the managers of all the theaters. Acts that came to London Thursday, Friday, and Saturday had no place to go on Sunday as the theaters were closed. We always had show people at our house on Sunday. Dad arranged for Isham Jones to come to our house after they finished at the Winter Garden. We had spaghetti and keg beer. It was one of the hottest days of the summer. It was Guy's birthday, and I remember we opened all the windows. The song that Isham Jones had just written was either 'Swinging Down the Lane' or 'I'll See You in My Dreams.' I always say it was first played by his pianist, Elridge, on our upright piano on Horton Street.

"We stayed up all night. It was a big affair. The whole of Isham Jones' band was there. He had a great big Indian tuba player, and the boys had just gotten a tuba player who was just learning. This Indian was one of the best tuba players around so he took our tuba player, Eddie Mashurette, for three or four days and taught him."

That night was a big one for Lebert. His idol, Louis Panico, was trumpeter for Isham Jones' band. Panico advised Lebert to listen to him and others, but most of all to develop his own sound. Lebert took the advice, as we all know, to heart.

Inspired, energetic, ambitious, and filled with the urge to travel and succeed, the Lombardo brothers turned their eyes in the direction of Cleveland, just across the lake from Port Stanley. But although they would live in the United States for the rest of their lives, their hearts would stay in Ontario. As Lebert says, "That was our last year in London, 1923."

3 The Lombardos Leave Home

☆ ☆ ☆ ☆ ☆ ☆ ☆ ☆ ☆ ☆ ☆ ☆

Chircosta

An early promotion photo of Guy Lombardo.

The Lombardos were out to conquer the world. They were riding high on a crest of popularity around London and didn't realize just how hard it was going to be to make the jump south of the border. Of course, Isham Jones had heard them play, but they still needed an American booker and that proved difficult. Guy, the eldest brother and the bandleader, set out to find a way to get bookings in the United States. Help came in the form of Corinne Arbuckle, a young singer who was doing a tour of provincial towns.

She'd belted out her songs for a few nights at London's Loews Theatre, and Guy had become enchanted with her. He set out to meet her. Corinne was kind and polite to the twenty-one-year-old bandleader and came over to the Winter Garden to listen to what was then called the Guy Lombardo Band. She was impressed but, as she candidly told the disappointed boys, as a singer she was hardly a big enough name to take a band along with her. She was sorry, she said, but she just couldn't help. Guy never took No for an answer in all his life, and this stubbornness proved to be one of his greatest assets. He begged Corinne, couldn't she at least give him the name of her booker? Corinne, remembering her first days perhaps (she wasn't too far ahead to have forgotten them), gave in. Her booker's name, she said, was Mike Shea, and he lived in Cleveland. Guy again persisted. He asked Shea to get him a job, any job. Guy pointed out that the boys were willing to work hard, and they knew they would have to start at the rock bottom. Couldn't he find them anything? Shea found them exactly one job. If the boys wanted, he would book them in a vaudeville club, the Elks Club, in Cleveland. Like conquering heroes, the boys boarded a bus for Cleveland amid the cheers and tears of their London friends and relatives. They appeared with eight other acts, one of which was a trained seal!

When Shea said it was a job for one night only, he wasn't kidding. The boys soon found themselves back in London, chagrined and embarrassed.

Guy again appealed to Mike Shea, and Shea came up with a one-week job in Akron, Ohio. The audience reaction wasn't too bad, and the man who owned the hall owned a theater as well. If the boys would play the dancehall by night and the theater by day, they could stay another week. This week gave Guy the chance to achieve one of his goals. He went down to radio station WTAM in Cleveland and offered to play on the air for free. Guy was convinced that if he could get his band on radio, they could be successful. He was right. The few radio broadcasts brought in a sprinkling of fan mail, letters Lebert has kept to this very day. He still has a scrapbook chock full of fan mail the band has received over the years and the early ones are his favorites. Incidentally, the Royal Canadians still receive thousands of fan letters each year. Their office staff in New York pass letters on to the individual band members, and they are almost as eagerly read as the mail fifty years ago.

Shea was impressed with the fan mail and set up the band on a five-week vaudeville tour with Corinne. After that tour, the boys would again be on their own.

Larry Owen, the joint owner and saxophonist of the Cleveland band, Vernon-Owen, told Guy about a new club due to open soon. It had been a speakeasy and had been closed by the law. It was due to reopen as a legitimate club. The owner, Louis Bleet, an immaculate, cultured, middle-aged man was obviously not impressed with Guy, but he saw the band in Akron and agreed to think about letting them open his club. On February 18th, 1924, the band opened the Claremont Inn under their new name.

It was their booker Shea's idea that they change their name. After all, the Guy Lombardo Band wasn't very distinctive. Shea thought they needed a more colorful name. Out of the discussions, the name Guy Lombardo and the Royal Canadians was born.

The band in 1928 consisted of the nine originals from London: the three Lombardos, Freddie Kreitzer on piano, George Gowans on drums, Francis Henry on guitar, Eddie Mashurette on tuba, Jeff Dillon on trombone, and Archie Cunningham on sax. "When we moved to Cleveland we had a funny thing," Freddie recalls. "The whole bunch of us had to have one room or we wouldn't check into a hotel."

During the four years the band played in Cleveland, the membership would change only slightly, resulting in a set of "first men" that, with additions, would remain together until the late 1940s.

Archie Cunningham decided after the vaudeville tour that he wanted to go home to London. He was replaced by one of Carmen's saxophone students, seventeen-year-old Fred Higman. In order not to confuse the two Freds, Fred Higman was called Derf. The name has stuck to this day. A third saxophonist was recruited to form the famous Lombardo sax section. This was Larry Owen, the Cleveland boy who had suggested that Guy go talk with Louis Bleet about the Claremont Inn. Larry was the first American to join the Lombardo band. The third change in the band happened when Eddie Mashurette became sick, returned home, and left an empty tuba chair. The recruitment was Bern Davies, another one of Carmen's saxophone students from back in London. "Mr. Lombardo, Papa, phoned and said they would like me to join the band," he recalls. "They wanted me to play tuba, an instrument I'd never seen." Papa took Bern to see Professor Vanuta, the man who had taught the brothers just a few years before, and soon he was playing tuba.

Even when there were great enticements, the original members felt such loyalty that they remained with the band. Freddie Kreitzer, the first non-Lombardo to join, was tempted in 1930 by an offer made to him by his father-in-law. Freddie says, "He wanted to set me up and a very fine French chef who was a friend of his in a place out on Long Island. I was supposed to be the greeter and play the piano. But I had always been with the band and I liked it so I stayed."

Bern Davies remembers the Claremont Inn vividly. "Louis Bleet was very nice and he ran a good show. They had a casino out in the back with a crap game and roulette. It was in Avon Park."

"It was one room with a small dance floor," Freddie adds. "The Claremont Inn was a place where we started work at seven-thirty or eight at night and played until one or two in the morning."

In the summers, the band played at the Lake Road Inn, also owned by Louis Bleet. His partner, who chose the acts, was Sophie Tucker. She heard the band at the Claremont and liked them, their first brush with stardom! "The Lake Road Inn was pretty nice," George Gowans explains. "Out in the country, one of those steak

Courtesy of Sam Fink

One of the band's original saxophone players, Derf Higman who was once a student of Carmen's, with his wife, Marietta, and the Lombardos' longtime London friends, Sam and Ruby Fink. Taken at the Roosevelt Grill.

places. The audiences were business people, lawyers and doctors."

Louis Bleet did more for the Royal Canadians than give them their first long-term job outside of Canada. Bleet loved music and knew that the young musicians were not employing their talents as well as they could. And so he guided them. Bleet told them to play more softly. He pointed out that an audience *will* listen to a band if it is good and not distracting. This advice has always stayed with the band. It *is* possible to listen to the band and talk at the same time without having to compete with the music. Bleet also told the band members to play soft chords under the solos. Until then, the members not playing had clapped an accompaniment to the solos. Most important, Bleet was the originator of the musical medley. Patrons had been complaining to Bleet that Guy had not played all the numbers they requested. Guy simply stated that the band didn't have enough time in one evening to fulfill every request. Bleet suggested the band play only *part* of each number, stringing four or five songs together. The medley was born.

Later, the Royal Canadians would leave the Claremont Inn and move to a club named the Music Box. Bleet had taught them much, but they had been unable to get a radio station to put a wire into

The children of Lebert's second marriage: Peter, Bill, and Susan Ann.

the Claremont because of its former reputation as a speakeasy. "The Music Box was a hard job," Freddie says. "We worked a noon session, dinner session, and a late night session. They had a habit of doing these noon sessions around Ohio."

In 1926, the brothers played the Blossom Heath, a snappy roadhouse on Lake Erie that had once been the Cleveland Yacht Club. Here they lived in tents. It was a happy bachelor life and they met all the girls of the Cleveland smart set. It was here that all three brothers met their wives, three beautiful girls from the Cleveland area. Florence Haas was to be Carmen's wife and remain with him all his life. Lilliebell Glen, still living in retirement on Long Island, married Guy. Lebert married a young girl, Carol Williams, who was to die seven years later.

Courtesy of Michael Nagro

Guy Lombardo and Al Quadbach, forty years after their first meeting in Chicago.

In 1927, Guy began receiving calls from a Chicago lawyer named Billy Stein, co-owner with his brother Jules, an eye doctor, of a booking agency named Music Corporation of America. The brothers wanted to sign up the band. Guy wasn't interested in joining MCA as Lebert explains: "We had everything in Cleveland, clubs, weddings, and school dances, so we didn't want to tie with MCA. Why should we pay them a commission? So Guy used to hang up on Bill Stein. All of a sudden Bill came to Cleveland and we took a liking to him. He even lived with us. Finally one day he got Guy to sign the contract with MCA. But Guy said, 'Now listen Bill, you don't get any commission while we're in Cleveland.' "

But Stein wanted Guy Lombardo's Royal Canadians in Chicago and so he brought to meet them a man described by those who knew him as a big, flashy, loudmouth Dutchman. His name was Al Quadbach and he owned a Chicago club called the Granada.

Quadbach offered the band $1,600 a week and said they would only have to play nights. The deal was struck.

Mama and Papa were not at all happy about their boys moving

as far away as Chicago. It had been safe when they were in Cleveland, under the eye of Mama's sister who lived there, and just across Lake Erie from London. But Chicago! Gangsters! No, Mama and Papa weren't happy at all. But after all, the brothers weren't really "their boys" anymore. They were Guy, Carmen, and Lebert, three mature men with wives.

The musicians themselves were sorry to leave Cleveland, but they weren't afraid of Chicago rowdyism at all. "They fought amongst themselves," George Gowans says of the Chicago gunmen. Bern Davies remembers the band members' early contact with gangsters while they were still in Cleveland. "There were a lot of gangsters there that we knew very well—they're still well-known figures in Las Vegas I believe—and we used to go out and drink with them. The music business is a funny thing. The guys that are the wildest, the gangsters, for some strange reason like musicians."

And so, in the autumn of 1927, the Royal Canadians moved to Chicago and started to play at Al Quadbach's club, the Granada, formerly called the Gingham Café. Lebert recalls, "Well, it was a little nightclub at Sixtieth Street and Cottage Grove, right opposite the biggest graveyard you ever saw in your life. This was an out-and-out joint!" Maybe it was, but Quadbach wanted the band and he had money.

Quadbach treated the club as his personal place to view what he considered the best band around, Guy Lombardo's Royal Canadians. Accordingly, he didn't bother to do any advertising for his club. For two months the band played to an empty house night after night as Quadbach contentedly leaned back in his chair and demanded the band play his favorite songs, "Melancholy Baby" and "What Can I Say After I Say I'm Sorry?"

"There was no business," Lebert remembers. "Nobody knew Guy Lombardo. So we played there night after night. No good. No one. So we said, 'It's no good here; we'll go to Kansas City.' "

But Quadbach wouldn't hear of that. He liked the band, wanted them to stay and was willing to do anything to get them to change their minds. Guy laid down the conditions: he had found, he told Quadbach, that radio was the way to get people to come to hear the band. Either Quadbach got a wire into the club or the Royal Canadians were leaving. That didn't give Quadbach a lot of choice, so he went ahead and made arrangements. Station WBBM, the newest Chicago station, so new that it hadn't even officially received its license, agreed to put the Royal Canadians on for fifteen minutes a night. On a winter night in November, the disillusioned band struck up their music, played to an empty house, and opened up the

Courtesy of MCA

The original band in an early promotion picture.

radio microphone. After the fifteen-minute broadcast, the tiny station was deluged with calls demanding more of the Lombardo music. Every time Guy announced it was time to sign off, WBBM's phone lines would be jammed. The band started at the beginning of their repertoire again (they hadn't counted on playing so long that night) and played until one in the morning.

People arrived at the club to see the band they were hearing on the radio. The boys were elated. Quadbach, on the other hand, was a bit annoyed. Customers meant he had to work and that he just couldn't sit back, relax, and hear his two favorite numbers played over and over.

The band members were afraid that the night was just a fluke. The next morning they found out otherwise. Mr. Florsheim of shoe fame and Mr. Wrigley of chewing gum fame both contacted Guy the next day. Each wanted to sponsor a half-hour weekly show live on the station. Guy Lombardo's Royal Canadians had jumped overnight from nobodies to moderate fame. Guy had been proved right again. The radio wire was the ticket to success. Mr. Wrigley, in fact, loved the Royal Canadians so much that he had their show piped out to a California station so that he could hear it on his estate on Catalina Island!

It has been said over the years that Quadbach was one of the "mob," a gangster. But all evidence points to the contrary. He was an explosive, impulsive man, but not a gangster. However, since many of his clientele were of that ilk, he learned to deal with them over the years.

Bern Davies remembers the gangster clientele good-naturedly. "When you're young, you don't really notice this. I know I used to go to the men's room and they'd be in there, three or four of them. They were always well dressed you know, nails manicured to the nth degree." He continues, "I'd be in the men's room combing my hair and they'd come in and pull two guns out from under their arms. They carried them in holsters under their arms. They'd lay them in front of them where they were washing so they wouldn't have to drag them out if things got rough. They *always* had the pistols up on the shelves. I was in there, we all were of course, and didn't think anything of it."

Still, there was one night in the Granada when the gangsters couldn't be ignored. Shortly before Christmas, 1927, on an evening when the Royal Canadians were giving an Al Jolson night, a gangster named George Maloney grabbed the microphone from Guy and tried to sing an Irish ballad. Guy escorted the man, who was very drunk, off the stage and gave him a shove to persuade him not to come up again. Quadbach quieted Maloney down and told Guy not to worry. But Guy did worry. After all, Maloney was a member of an Irish gang that wanted to oust Al Capone and his gang from their powerful position in Chicago crime.

On the Sunday after Christmas, Mama, Papa, and Elaine were visiting the boys in the Granada Café. That night Maloney decided to return. Guy was onstage reading telegrams sent to him via radio station WBBM's Nutty Club. To be a member, Guy had to read your telegram onstage. Suddenly shots were heard as Maloney unloaded his revolver into two members of a rival gang who had been kidding him about being thrown off the stage by Guy a few days before. The two men died instantly, each with one bullet in his head and one in his heart. The audience dived under the tables and the band members hit the floor. Guy yelled at Freddie to play, play anything. Freddie started playing "She's Funny That Way," and Guy, dumbfounded by the situation yet realizing that he was on live radio, started to sing. It was the only time he sang in public in his long career.

Later the full story came out. Maloney had come in unarmed, but after being ribbed, had lost his temper and sent his girlfriend out to the parking lot to get his revolver from under the front seat of his car. Maloney fled after the murder—his girlfriend stayed behind in the Granada—but was soon caught by police. Many years later Guy told the story to a journalist who asked, "Was he executed for the shootings?" Guy replied, "No, about a year later he got off on a plea of self-defense. Then they machine-gunned him down on the street, but that didn't kill him either, just filled him full of holes. Then he heard they were going to kill him in hospital, so he escaped from there. Later, I heard he died of pneumonia."

This was the first time a murder had been broadcast live on radio.

When the author's great-uncle was married in Chicago, he took his bride to the Granada Café. There, Guy congratulated him on his marriage and, jesting that the young man had seen the last of his bachelor days, played the tune "Ready for the River."

It was in Chicago that the Lombardo brothers first met their friend Louis Armstrong. "I'll tell you about when I first met Louis," Lebert says. "He was playing in Chicago at a dancehall and we had Sunday nights off. I went over to the Savoy Ballroom to hear him play. You see, in those days colored people weren't allowed in the Granada, and all the colored musicians, like Louis and Cab Calloway, used to come to the parking lot, and we'd open the high windows so they could hear the band. They loved the sound of the saxophones. So one night I was over at the Savoy where Louis was playing and he said, 'Gee, I'd like to hear the band.' So I said, 'OK, Louis, after work tonight, we play till three o'clock, come on over.' Later that night one of the dishwashers said, 'There's a colored guy out there who wants to see you.' So I went out and it was Louis. So I said to him, 'Follow me.' Well, our bandstand was out front and there were two swinging doors into the kitchen and in behind was Al Quadbach's office and our room. So I brought Louis across the dance floor and into our room. There was a knock on the door and it was Al. 'Get that guy out of here!' I said, 'Al, please, he's a friend of mine. Don't embarrass me!' 'Get him out of here!' Al screamed. Al had two hates, colored people and Chicago musicians. Isn't that a quirk? "So anyway," Lebert continues, "I made up some cock-and-bull story and I led Louis back out. But I was never so embarrassed. I saw Louis so many, many times before he died and he never even mentioned that. Louis Armstrong was a wonderful person."

Partly as a result of this incident, the Lombardo brothers decided to hold a special concert so that everyone who wanted to hear them could come. It was held in the South Side Armory of Chicago, and 20,000 cheering fans showed up. The Royal Canadians played tunes such as "Tiger Rag," "When the Saints Go Marching In," and "Star Dust." Guy always said it was one of the best concerts they ever did.

Quadbach was fiercely loyal to "his boys," as he now called the Royal Canadians. Bern Davies tells this story: "When we first started to work there we were in Quadbach's office and there was a music publisher that Carmen didn't like. Carmen was writing songs at that time. Carmen said, 'Who's that picture you've got there on the wall? Isn't that so-and-so?' And Al said 'Yeah.' Carmen said, 'Well, I don't like him!' All of a sudden there was the most deafening roar. Al had whipped out a pistol and blown the picture off the wall!"

Chicago reviewer, Ashton Stevens, after seeing the Royal Canadians at the Palace Theater, coined a phrase that, slightly altered, remains with the band to this very day. He called the band "the softest and sweetest jazzmen on any stage this side of heaven." Out of these words grew the slogan "The sweetest music this side of heaven."

Guy Lombardo and his brothers were happy in Chicago, but Jules Stein planned to make them even happier. And so, Jules arranged for the band to move to New York City. The brothers and the band members were sorry to leave Al. They had grown fond of him. He had treated them as his own sons and showered them with presents. One Christmas he gave every band member a set of diamond cuff links.

Still, the opportunity to move to New York was too good to refuse. Although Al cajoled and pleaded, he finally had to give up his fight to keep the Royal Canadians in Chicago.

4 New York, New Years!

On October 3, 1929, the Royal Canadians moved to New York City. Shortly after the band made their debut at the Roosevelt Grill, the stock market crashed. The band had spent the day in the recording studio, and one of the songs set to wax had been "My Fate Is in Your Hands." The Lombardo brothers lost heavily on that Black Thursday. Guy lost about $60,000 in the few short hours during which his Cities Service Gas Company stock plunged from eighty cents to fourteen.

For a while the crash emptied the grill of its rich New York patrons and out-of-town businessmen. But soon a new audience, younger than before, swelled to hear the Lombardos. So while men threw themselves off window ledges after losing a fortune, and women and children cried themselves to sleep at night, the stock market crash did not hurt the band's musical career. "To be truthful, it didn't do much," Freddie Kreitzer recalls. "After a couple of broadcasts we had that place packed every night. We drew from Yale, Harvard, and Brown, and those kids used to come in their full-dress suits, and it was a beautiful sight to see."

The Lombardos had chosen wisely when they decided to make the Roosevelt Grill their permanent winter home. The atmosphere of the grill suited their music and clientele. Designed by brother Joe, who now owns an interior design and antique business in Manhatten, the two-tiered room with its second dance floor offered patrons either a quiet evening for two or a crowded dance floor

Courtesy of Alec Davidson

The ROOSEVELT GRILL
The Winter Home of Guy Lombardo
Madison Avenue at 45th Street, New York 17

where everyone enjoyed tunes such as "Ain't Misbehavin', " "June Moon," or "Moanin' Low." By this time Guy had proved himself to be a good judge of what an audience wanted, and for the Roosevelt he chose what today we would call schmaltz. Then, it was just plain mood or emotion. With the mood of the song Guy would change the color of the room so that "Deep Purple" would bathe the dancers in deep purple light and "Soft Lights and Sweet Music" would bring on soft pinks and roses. The band began the dinner music at seven in the evening and switched to dance music at nine.

When the Royal Canadians played at the Roosevelt Grill, the place was always crowded. Alec Davidson remembers, "I used to listen to the people and their comments. This could be a Monday night and the place would be fairly crowded, and I heard musicians who were going on to their jobs later, and they would say, 'I don't know what the magic is, but the guy can bring them in here every night.' "

For the small-town London boys, the climb to the top—New York—had been hard work, but they had always been in the right place at the right time and only six years had gone by since they had tearfully hugged Mama and Papa good-bye at the London, Ontario railway station. From this point on, the Lombardo brothers would never suffer financially. There would be setbacks, mostly due to failing business enterprises not related to music, but they always had their talent for music and they would recoup. By the spring of 1930 the Lombardos were making twenty-five percent of the profits of the Roosevelt Grill, their share averaging about $7,500 a week. Guy was only twenty-eight at the time and this was the depression!

The brothers settled into New York, each renting an apartment in Manhattan. Brother Joe decorated Guy's apartment and this was the beginning of a fruitful relationship between the two brothers. Joe would later decorate Guy's other homes and Guy's East Point House Restaurant. In fact, through Guy, Joe got to know many bandleaders, politicians, and show-biz personalities. Both Perry Como and Governor Rockefeller used Joe's expertise. Elaine Gardner points to a chair in the living room and laughs, "That was Tommy Dorsey's chair. Joe got it while redecorating and I just had to have it." George Gowans, Derf Higman, and Freddie Kreitzer were not married at this time, and true to their Cleveland style, they shared an apartment.

In the early 1940s the four brothers moved to Long Island and built their permanent homes. Carmen settled in Woodmere; Victor and his first wife, Ginny, in Oak Beach; Lebert in Manhasset; and Guy in Freeport. The brothers were within a half-hour drive of

Courtesy of Kenny Gardner

Guy takes a tumble on Carmen's backyard rink.

Courtesy of Mr. and Mrs. Kenny Gardner

Carmen welcomes visitors to his house on Long Island where, Canadian style, the family enjoyed a backyard skating rink.

each other. Mama and Papa, with brother Joe and sisters Elaine and Rosemarie, were only an hour away in Connecticut.

In 1929, the Lombardo band, by then so popular that two radio networks wanted their services, ushered out the old year for CBS and rang in the new year for NBC. As CBS closed its show at midnight, the opening announcement was read on NBC. A tradition was born that December 31, and the band has never missed a New Year's broadcast.

If the Lombardo brothers and the Royal Canadians have carved a niche in North America that is theirs forever, it is certainly with the song "Auld Lang Syne." It has become such a North American tradition to listen to the Royal Canadians playing the song on New Year's Eve that even those who really don't like the Lombardo sound, or who call Guy the King of Corn, feel a burst of nostalgia and reverently watch the band count down the seconds to a sparkling new year. Even *Life* magazine commented, "Should Guy Lombardo and his Royal Canadians fail to play 'Auld Lang Syne' at midnight, New Year's Eve, a deep uneasiness would run through a large segment of the American populace, a conviction that despite the evidence on every calendar, the new year has not really arrived."

The Lombardo brothers have always been mystified that everyone thought it so brilliant of them to think up the idea of playing that song on New Year's Eve. "To us," Guy said, "it was always so

Courtesy of Kenny Gardner

Members of the Lombardo family and band enjoy the ice at Carmen's Long Island home.

natural, it came without thinking." Way back in 1914 and 1915 when Guy, Carmen, and Lebert were driving around the London countryside in the Studebaker with Mama and Papa, the old Scottish songs "Auld Lang Syne" and "Comin' thro' the Rye," both written by Robert Burns, were beloved of the largely Scottish rural population. The songs have been part of their repertoire ever since.

Burns wrote the song "Auld Lang Syne" in 1788, but its words and meaning of "old long since" or "the good old days" are timeless. The melody, some say, is an old Scottish tune known as "The Miller's Wedding." Others claim that William Shield used something very close to the melody in his opera *Rosina* which was presented at the Covent Garden Opera House in London, England, in 1783. Perhaps Burns heard the melody there.

Whatever the song's origin, it has come to be sung to end parties at the close of the night. The singers stand in a circle, cross their arms in front of their chests, hold their neighbors' arms, and sway back and forth singing of their friendship with each other. As *Radio Stars* magazine pointed out, "It evokes a sense of the fragrance of the past, of old friendships that never die, of old loves always young, and of the bright colors of youthful dreams. Under its melody you can reach out, capture something old and lovely."

Except for the years 1933-1935, when New York Central Railroad which ran the Roosevelt lowered the Royal Canadians' fee

Guy Lombardo in his
most famous role,
genial New Year's host.

in order to bring it in line with musicians' union fees, the band
played their New Year's Eve broadcast from the Roosevelt until
1963. (The two years in the thirties saw the band broadcast from
California.) The following year, 1964, the Lombardo brothers
staged what is quite probably the biggest New Year's Eve bash ever
held in North America. Inspired by Mrs. Winthrop Rockefeller,
chairman of a charity ball in aid of the Mental Health Association
of New York, Carmen hired Grand Central Station for the night of
December 31. Heaters were installed, trains rerouted, and 2,000
people dined on caviar and champagne while viewers on several
hundred television stations watched. A ticket for that evening was
$400 or $1,000 if one wanted to sit near the band. All in all, more
than $20,000 was raised for the charity.

After 1964 the New Year's Eve broadcasts came live from the
Waldorf-Astoria in New York City. Lebert, laughing, remembers
one broadcast vividly. "I'll never forget that night. We were on the
air and it was so cold you have no idea. But the pipes let go and it
was raining cats and dogs! Nobody could see it on television. They
moved everything over. But the women had their furs and clothes
all drenched."

During the Royal Canadians' first year in New York, another
Lombardo joined the band. That was brother Victor, who played
clarinet and saxophone. Victor had a band of his own that played in
London, Cleveland, and Toronto. Guy wasn't so sure that he
wanted Victor in the band just because his name was Lombardo,
but he agreed to let Victor come and try. Vic arrived, sans sax
which he had hocked along the way, and the three elder brothers
were shocked. Little brother Vic was good—darn good—and he
became a Royal Canadian. Unfortunately, Victor was later to
disagree with his brothers over money and not being allowed to be a
partner in the ownership of the band and so left several times to
form his own orchestra. Because unscrupulous dancehall managers
often advertised Victor's band as an adjunct of Guy's, it was hard
for him to be independent. Victor came back to the Royal Canadians shortly before Guy died and left again after New Year's Eve,
1978. At the present time, Victor again has his own band and is
based in Florida.

The Lombardos began their first across-the-nation radio show in
1930. On NBC, live from the Roosevelt Grill, on Monday nights
from seven to seven-thirty PM, the Robert Burns Panatella Cigar
Show was to bring the Royal Canadians and popular music into the
living rooms of all America. Every week the band introduced a Hit
of the Week on the program. Carmen and Guy would screen all the

Courtesy of Alec Davidson

Christmas cards
designed by the
Lombardos' old friend,
Alec Davidson.

new songs and narrow the selection down to two or three. Then the Royal Canadians as a whole would vote, and their decision would determine a song and songwriter's future. Guy was well aware of the power he had to make a songwriter's future bright. "In 1928 or 1929 I introduced 'You're Driving Me Crazy' on a Saturday night on the network and by Wednesday night it was the biggest song in the country," Guy once said.

In 1933 Guy decided to try putting a comedy team on the Robert Burns Show. Comics were having a hard time adjusting from vaudeville to radio. Standing in a glass booth and reading his lines seemed to make a comic lose his punch. Guy suggested putting a live audience in the studio and, with this historic suggestion, opened up the world of radio to such giants as Jack Benny, George Burns, and Gracie Allen. When Guy chose to put George Burns and Gracie Allen on his show, the audience was furious at first that the comedy team took time away from the Lombardo music. Then Guy hit on the idea of having the music play softly underneath the comics. The idea took hold and George Burns and his famous cigar made the sponsors very happy.

Because of the Lombardos' immense popularity and access to broadcast time, the band became a favorite target for the song pluggers and songwriters of Tin Pan Alley. Guy set an iron policy from the start. No amount of show tickets, liquor, women, money, or free vacations would induce the Royal Canadians to play a song. The band would only play a song they liked and it had to be good. So no bribes please! A band could only maintain a first-class image if it always played first-class songs, Guy reasoned.

Guy also made it clear that the regular late-night rehearsals were closed. "Everybody in the band had a word in these rehearsals," Freddie says. "It wasn't a matter of Guy or Carmen saying, 'We'll do it this way.' We used to talk everything over. We'd say, 'Well, no, let's try it this way' or 'We'll do it that way.' " Sometimes it took a whole practice to work out a song until everyone was satisfied, but that was the Lombardo way. The arrangement had to be perfect.

Apart from these few ground rules, song pluggers and songwriters were welcome to come around to the Roosevelt with their songs. After all, a hit band needs hit songs. There was a music room at the back of the grill and the songwriters would come and play their tunes. George Gowans remembers, "The back of the bandstand would be full of song pluggers wanting the Lombardo band to introduce their songs on the air. It happened every week so you got used to it, you didn't mind it. I don't think there were any special writers. If the song was good it got played."

Every Royal Canadian who is asked about songwriters mentions Irving Berlin and Walter Donaldson. "Irving Berlin and Walter Donaldson were good friends of ours," Bern Davies says. "They would bring all their songs into the back room. Berlin played and so did Donaldson, badly, but they did play piano, and they would demonstrate their own songs. They usually would give us three months before anyone else had them. Berlin songs such as 'Alexander's Ragtime Band,' 'Easter Parade,' 'White Christmas,' 'When I Lost You,' and 'Oh, How I Hate to Get Up in the Morning' are well known today. So are Donaldson songs such as 'Little White Lies,' 'Yes Sir, That's My Baby,' and 'At Sundown.'

"Donaldson was an excellent songwriter," Davies remembers. "He was also an impulsive gambler. He used to go to Las Vegas and friends would say, 'It's idiotic for you to go gambling. The wheels are fixed. There's no way you can win.' By gosh, an hour after he got there he lost all his money on the wheel. He was like Ted Lewis, the King of Jazz, the high-hat guy with the clarinet, who persisted for years and years. One week in Las Vegas and Lewis would be in hock for six months."

When asked if Berlin or Donaldson ever disapproved of his arrangements, Dewey Bergman, the Royal Canadians' arranger since 1937 replies, "Thank God, no! I once took down a song from Berlin over the telephone during the ASCAP fight [see p. 57]. I made the lead sheet and then I made the arrangement. It was the last day we could record and we were in the studio all day at Decca. It wasn't a hit song."

Dewey Bergman has been involved in music all his life. He was a friend of Scott Joplin's and as a youngster used to play ragtime music with him. Of his long association with the Royal Canadians, which still exists today, Bergman says, "I did all their arranging and record production. Boyd Bunch was with the band before me. I really took his place. I made a study of the sound of the band and the limitations of their range on their instruments. Guy had a very good ear for what the public liked. Before I was with him I was with CBS as head arranger. I did different types of things there. But with Guy's brass section, he would never let you go over a certain note that would hurt the public's ear."

Guy placed many restrictions on Bergman. "People think it was an easy band to write for, but it was probably the most difficult. I'm the only one who got Guy to update anything. I changed tempos on him. I used to bring in songs on my own and put them in the back of the book." Bergman cites the beguine or Latin beat as an example. He says that at first Guy refused to play the tempo, claiming that it would make his band sound too much like that of Xavier Cugat. Finally, persuaded by the band members and Bergman, Guy tried the tempo out on the dancers at the Roosevelt Grill, and they loved it. "From then on he played it eight times a night," Bergman says. "When he liked something, he'd drive you crazy with it!"

Audiences over the years have grown to love Bergman's arrangements. The shimmering saxes, the muted trumpets, and clear twin pianos (each playing a separate arrangement) are warmly familiar today. Bergman's most recent arrangement for the Royal Canadians is a version of "Don't It Make My Brown Eyes Blue." It is one of the most popular songs with the band's current road audiences.

Another interesting character from the early Roosevelt era was Johnny Meyer who met them just before they left Chicago. He was able to give the brothers good tips on the stock market and direct them toward good prices no matter what they wanted to buy. Johnny was good to the brothers and even found the Connecticut home for Guy's parents when Mama and Papa decided to move closer to their boys after the sudden death of Lebert's first wife in 1934. Johnny even lived with Lebert for a time. Later Johnny hooked up with Errol Flynn and, after Flynn died, became an intimate of Aristotle Onassis. He was one of those rare individuals who could fit in with anyone simply because he knew so many people and had experienced so much.

Today Lebert speaks of Tin Pan Alley and the early years the Lombardos spent in New York this way: "It was a beehive. It was really great. I mean every firm had their representatives that would contact the different orchestra leaders, and we were known to introduce new songs on the air. We had that reputation. But that's all gone . . ."

5 Thirty Years of the Sweetest Music

The Lombardo brothers owned a music publishing business during the late 1930s and early 1940s. It wasn't called Lombardo Publishing because orchestra leaders supposedly didn't tinker in the business end of music. Instead the firm was named Olman Publishing after Abe Olman, the manager.

Guy's sister Elaine was the secretary of the business and she remembers the excitement of Tin Pan Alley. "Being a secretary, I worked for Guy's firm. I was always in the back room with Miss Connie who made out the payroll for the band. But I didn't like it back there. I liked it up in the front where all the songwriters and singers came in. It was so exciting! We had little rooms the singers could use and we had a coach, a piano player who would rehearse singers. We would gladly rehearse a singer if he was going to do our song. In the front room we gave out 'black and whites' or professional copies of the music. So the songwriters and orchestra leaders made the rounds of the Brill Building where we and all the other music publishers were."

In 1939 the Royal Canadians were doing a radio show for CBS called "The Lady Esther Show." Because Carmen hated to sing, Guy had been trying out guest vocalists on the show in order to relieve his brother. Elaine answered the band's fan mail in her job as secretary. Every time a guest singer appeared on the show, the fans would write in to complain, she recalls, and demand that Carmen go back to being singer as well as saxophonist.

An early publicity shot.

Through Elaine, however, the Royal Canadians were to find the vocalist that suited the music and delighted their fans. The year was 1939, and the singer's name was Kenny Gardner.

Kenny had been raised in a little town in Nebraska. His family, unlike Guy's, had been in North America a long time. "My family were just plain Yankee-Doodle-uptown-Mayflower types. They came to this country so long ago they've got towns named after them—like Gardner, Massachusetts. They moved out first to the Ohio area after it got crowded in New England and when they got to Ohio they dropped the *i* from the name. It used to be Gardiner. Then that branch went on straight west and kept the name Gardner. That's me. But those that went southwest, down into Texas, got lazier yet and dropped the *d* and became Garner. Vice-President Garner is part of the clan." Kenny laughs. "Now that doesn't mean that we don't have just as many horse thieves in the family."

Lanky and blond, with a rich, romantic voice, Kenny did not have training as a singer. "Well, when it came to music, I liked it. I never had training in it, but unlike most singers who got into it either because they had musical training, came from stage families, or wrote songs, I sang simply because I liked the songs and I liked to sing them. It was fun. If somebody wanted to pay me that was fine, but I was having a ball. This has been my whole philosophy as far as the music business is concerned."

After leaving Nebraska, Kenny had gone to California to become an engineer, but had begun singing in nightclubs. Soon he was on staff at NBC, doing a regular nightly show, called "Easy Does It," from seven to seven-thirty PM. In those days radio networks had staff singers and musicians. NBC had three regular, young male singers: Bill Johnson in New York, Johnny Johnson in Chicago, and Kenny in Hollywood. When Bill Johnson decided to leave NBC to join a group, a coin was tossed and Kenny landed in New York. Before he left California, Kenny went to see his orchestra leader at NBC, Gordon Jenkins, a fine composer and conductor whose orchestra did the famous recording of Artie Shaw's "Frenesi." Jenkins told Kenny to go to the Brill Building in New York to the firm of Bergman, Vacco, and Kahn. Music publishers took singers under their wing at this time, and that firm was to be Kenny's main contact with the music world. Kenny went to the Brill Building, took the elevator to the ninth floor, and entered the firm of Olman Publishing by mistake. There he met Elaine. Over the next few months, Kenny often stopped by to chat with Elaine, remarking that he didn't like New York and wanted to go back to California.

Kenny had a right to be anxious. Shortly after he arrived in New York, NBC and CBS jointly decided that they didn't want to pay the American Society of Composers, Authors and Publishers (ASCAP) any more money than they were already paying for the use of their songwriters' songs. (ASCAP is the agency that collects and distributes royalties on behalf of musicians.) The two networks formed their own company, Broadcast Music Incorporated, or BMI. Kenny tells of the problem: "They called me in at NBC and said, 'Kenny, you know of course that we are having an argument with ASCAP, and we've set up our own music publishing company. Starting next week, one quarter of the tunes you sing on air have to be published by our new company.' But 'Jeannie with the Light

Brown Hair' was about all they had. So the week after that they called me in and said, 'Kenny, that show was all right. Now you've got to go fifty percent BMI.' The next week they told me it was now one hundred percent. 'Well,' I said, 'that's all well and good, but now I've got you. Where am I going to get the material?' "

That was a fair question on Kenny's part. NBC, as he says, "was paying his freight," but the ASCAP songwriters were seasoned, respected, and he drew on them heavily. He had a nightly half-hour show to fill. NBC gave him the address on Fifth Street of the new BMI office. Kenny relates: "Here they have an office about the size of this house, and they had every amateur songwriter in America. They must have spent millions of dollars to get black and whites made up. They had two kids, songwriters named Kramer and Whitney, who had written 'Far Away Places' and 'My Sister and I,' playing the piano and demonstrating songs. Mac David, the man who writes songs like 'Raindrops Keep Fallin' on My Head' with Burt Bacharach was there. There was Dinah Shore, Judy Holliday—in those days her name was Judith Tuvim—Compton and Green, and Jimmy Dorsey, all of us up there listening to these tunes. Usually you'd get about four bars in and throw them away, but we were able to keep going and picked a few good tunes, 'High on a Hill,' 'My Sister and I,' 'Symphony,' and we finally got enough tunes to make up a program. But it was murder!"

For the Royal Canadians, who of course did not know Kenny at this time, the ASCAP-BMI problem was just as serious. "We recorded one or two days before the ruling applied, all day, all day. We laid up a whole bunch of records before that strike started," Freddie Kreitzer says.

Elaine lived with her parents at their home in Stamford, Connecticut, which the brothers had bought as a present for them. Every day she left her car at the Connecticut station and took the train to New York City. When she got in her car to drive home, she always turned on the radio immediately. She knew the music business, was a part of it, and loved it. One day while she was driving home Elaine heard an unfamiliar voice singing. "We had a big circular driveway in front of the house. My mother came to the kitchen door, and I'm sitting in the car, and the voice is singing 'Mean to Me' or 'Am I Blue,' and Mama says, 'Aren't you coming in?' But I had to find out who was singing. I was curious. Well, he did his own announcing and I couldn't believe that this guy Kenny Gardner who came into the office had such a nice voice—real romantic."(As she tells the story to the author, her husband, Kenny, blushes at this part and says, "Go on, Elaine, go on!")

A family gathering at
Mama's and Papa's
house in Connecticut.

Courtesy of Lebert Lombardo

Courtesy of Mr. and Mrs. Kenny Gardner

Christmas at Mama and Papa Lombardo's Connecticut house,
probably in 1950. Kenny Gardner, kneeling, took the picture.

"Now you know the boys were at the Roosevelt and every Sunday Guy, Carmen, Lebert, and Vic, and their wives all came to Connecticut for Sunday dinner. My Mother and Dad were alone during the week. They just looked forward to the weekend. Sunday was the day. I did the baking and Mama did the cooking. It was a twenty-two room house and we had help, but Guy had certain friends in the music business that he liked so he would bring them along. We were always prepared. Thirty or thirty-five at the table didn't mean anything in that huge dining room.

"So it's getting around four o'clock on Sunday and Lee and Al Reiser were supposed to come on the radio, but there was a change and Kenny came on instead. He was what they term 'on call.' He lived at the Belmont Plaza and if NBC needed him they'd call. Right

Singer Kenny Gardner served in the Seventy-first Infantry in World War II. He married Elaine Lombardo in 1944.

after the show the car pulled up and Guy got out. I said, 'Did you have the radio on NBC?' He said, 'No. Why?' "

Elaine told him about Kenny, and the next day Guy asked his producer on "The Lady Esther Show," Ted Siston, to get an air check, or record, of Kenny. Guy was always at work at the Roosevelt at seven PM when Kenny was on the air and so had never heard him. Siston got the air check and Guy heard half of it and said, "He's for me!" So he sent a close friend of his and Carmen's named Stan Stanley, a song plugger from Chappell Music Publishing (which is still in existence today), to the Belmont to find Kenny. After all, Guy was fussy and he wanted the singer to be good-looking, well dressed, in short to make a good appearance. The next day Kenny showed up at Olman Publishing and found out Elaine's last name. She had discovered him!

Kenny sang with the Royal Canadians from 1940 to 1978 except for the war years. Having joined the Seventy-first Infantry unit as a private, he returned as a battalion commander.

During a leave from the army, on September 7, 1944, Kenny and Elaine were married. The wedding took place at brother Carmen's house on Long Island. Baby sister Rosemarie, then eighteen years old, was the bride's maid of honor. As friends remember, Elaine looked radiant in a pale blue ensemble with a corsage of purple orchids on her shoulder. After a short honeymoon in Connecticut, Kenny reported to Fort Benning in Georgia to work for Uncle Sam.

The singing position now left open was quickly taken up by a fifth Lombardo, baby Rosemarie. This was a hard time for a young girl to be on the road touring . It was wartime and accommodations, transportation, and food were not as easily found nor as comfortable as before. Female vocalists wore evening gowns then and after the band left the Roosevelt each spring and went on the road, Rosemarie would have to spend her afternoons ironing layers and layers of net. But Rosemarie was plucky and she plowed through the war years doing war benefits with the band as well as the season at the Roosevelt and touring. In 1943 she eloped with a young army lieutenant, but came back to continue singing. She was never happy being a singer and was only too glad to retire in 1948. Later she divorced the lieutenant and married a man in the hotel business from Toledo, Ohio, named Sid Rogers. They have three children, two boys and a girl, aged nineteen to twenty-three. She had never made it big as a singer, but her voice *was* good. It has been described as a pretty voice, contralto, or a "deep river" voice.

In 1949, when the Royal Canadians celebrated their twentieth anniversary at the Roosevelt, *Variety* magazine devoted a special issue to them. Perhaps of all the articles published that September 28, the biggest accolade came in an article written by Paul Whiteman, a man the three brothers had idolized many years before.

GUY SAYS I INSPIRED HIM
By Paul Whiteman

During a reception, following a concert of mine in Indianapolis several years ago, I chatted with a ballroom operator who had recently played Guy Lombardo and his Royal Canadians then on a spring tour of one-nighters. The ballroom had been so packed, the operator told me cheerily, that even a New York subway guard couldn't have jammed in any of the disappointed latecomers clamoring at the entrance. The box office was closed in an attempt to discourage them but they protested so noisily that the operator came out and explained that it wouldn't be fair to sell tickets since it was impossible to shoehorn another couple on the dance floor.

They didn't care whether or not they got on the floor, a lot of the people said. If they could only get inside and watch and listen to the famous music played in person they would feel repaid. Many had driven hundreds of miles for a glimpse of the band. There were so many fans and they were all so vehement, the operator said, that he felt that all of Indiana had nothing but Lombardo on his [sic] mind that night. He let in as many as he and the Fire Dept. dared and the rest had to wait their turn for others to leave, although almost no one went away until the final strains of "Auld Lang Syne," played by the most recognizable sax trio in the music business, floated across the room.

Now that's the sort of tribute that carries 10 times the weight of the fanciest testimonial dinner that any press agent ever dreamed up. Those people loved the Lombardo brand of music so much they were willing to travel great distances to hear it in person and though it's primarily meant to dance to, they were willing to sacrifice their place on the floor if they could be in the same room with it.

"I've told you this because I've always heard that your orchesta in the early twenties was Guy's inspiration," the operator said. My chest is pretty big but it swelled even bigger that night in Indianapolis.

The Switch

It wasn't the first time I'd heard the remark. Guy has told me that himself and, in a business in which a bandleader seldom credits another bandleader with anything except swiping his stuff, it's a refreshing thing to hear. This is especially true when you consider that the style of the Royal Canadians has been imitated more than that of all the other original stylists combined. Guy, however, has never been heard to make any unflattering comments about his imitators, even the ones who had their arrangers glued to a radio copying his orchestrations note for note.

Like Bing Crosby, Guy is an intense perfectionist and, like Bing, cloaks the fact with an easy, relaxed attitude that could be misinterpreted by casual observers as indifference. Guy could no more hold his huge and loyal following by being indifferent to the music than he could roll up speedboat records by being indifferent to the engine.

Guy's enthusiasm and drive has been matched by the same qualities in his brothers Carmen and Lebert; in Fred Kreitzer, his first pianist; in Dudley Fosdick in his brass section; in Derf Higman, the tenor sax man who spells his first name, Fred, backwards, and in others who played the opening night at the Roosevelt with Guy 20 years ago and who were Royal Canadians several years before that and still are with the band. During a rehearsal they all work and worry over each phrase, each brass figure and little fill-ins as if they were still kids preparing for their first important job. That's probably why all their jobs have been so important.

Come to think of it, Guy's claim that he plays the sweetest music this side of heaven may be too modest. After all, no one's ever proved there's a sweeter brand on the other side.

By 1952, the Royal Canadians, who had done so well on radio, followed the trend and entered the television era. At first they did a local show, shown in New York, which ran live once a week from the Roosevelt from seven to seven-thirty. It was sponsored by Lincoln-Mercury. By 1954, the Lombardos started a weekly, nationally syndicated series which they made at a private production studio with a group of dancers. Six shows were shot in one day, and this proved to be too much for the musicians who were no longer young men. "You couldn't do the two things," Kenny says. "It was plain murder. At the end of one session Derf collapsed. We would get off at the Roosevelt at two in the morning and we had to be ready to shoot in make-up at eight AM, which meant you had to be there at six-thirty or seven o'clock. It was obvious we couldn't do the two things and the live appearances at the Roosevelt were our first love." Later, color television made the black-and-white shows outdated, as were the clothes and hairdos of the dancers. The show was dropped in 1957. Times were changing . . .

Courtesy of Loblaws Limited

In the fifties, Loblaws sponsored the band and the band promoted Loblaws in Canada.

During the 1960s the entertainment scene in New York City was quickly changing too. Even the Roosevelt Grill, winter home of Guy's Royal Canadians since 1929, was coming under new management. It was doubtful that the Roosevelt could support the Royal Canadians in the new atmosphere.

Lady Luck has been a close companion of the Lombardos all their lives. In the winter of 1963, a superb opportunity was offered the brothers. A developer, Lou Belanti, from Harrison, New York, in conjunction with the oil-wealthy Murchison brothers from Texas, was building a huge housing, resort, and business complex named Tierra Verde near St. Petersburg, Florida. The group wanted the Royal Canadians to be the entertainment drawing card. Lebert gives us the history: "About a year before we became involved with Tierra Verde a consultant named Arthur Etkus called Guy about a boating project. He said, 'Guy, I have to go to Detroit. You'll help me out a lot if you come with me. I'll get you back in time for the show.' Guy went with him. Then a year later Lou Belanti called in the same consultant about Tierra Verde. He took a look at the place, liked it, and said 'Well, Mr. Belanti, all you need here is Guy Lombardo!'

"So the two of them flew to New York and called Guy. Etkus came out to the beach and he described Tierra Verde, how beautiful it was—and it is a beautiful spot—and sure enough they started to build the Port-O-Call where we played."

Original plans called for a small resort motel where people could stay when they came to visit Tierra Verde to investigate moving there permanently. When the Lombardo brothers decided to make the development their permanent winter home, the resort motel grew to 120 rooms and was named Guy Lombardo's Port-O-Call Inn and Country Club.

The Lombardos were offered fifty percent of all liquor and food profits from the Port-O-Call dining lounge. In addition, they were to receive a percentage from the homes sold in the development and free homes there until they could build their own. The Royal Canadian members received their usual pay. Guy, Carmen, Lebert, and all the band members could play their music while having their families with them in sunny Florida. It seemed ideal.

Tierra Verde, or Green Land, was an ambitious business project. In a beautiful setting, fifteen natural islands had been filled in and connected to form six. The advertising boasted miles of steel-reinforced concrete seawalls, wide and deep waterways, and the world's finest drainage system capable of draining off four inches of water an hour.

There were 6,000 waterfront and waterview sites available for homes, apartment buildings, and businesses. The developers promised that each home would be custom built and would have central air conditioning and heating. Homes would cost in the range of $20 thousand to $100 thousand.

The six-lane Pinellas Bayway system would connect the six Tierra Verde islands to St. Petersburg, only three-and-a-half miles away. The same highway leads to nearby Fort de Soto Park with its five miles of white beach, excursion tour train around the park, and Spanish-American fortress.

The Murchisons and Lou Belanti have a reputation for thoroughness and professionalism. As their advertising states, "Long before the first shovel dug into the ground, Tierra Verde was planned as a *perfect* community, down to the finest detail. Hotel property was zoned to face broad beaches and the western sunshine, residential property took advantage of the leeward side for year-round living . . . and each waterway was engineered to achieve the ideal in wind and tidal conditions."

Guy Lombardo's Royal Canadians filled the $5 million, 1,300-seat showplace Port-O-Call dining lounge night after night. "We were quite fancy there," Freddy Kreitzer recalls. "We had a couple of changes of coats." One of the uniform coats was canary yellow. The Port-O-Call was elegant and expansive, with beautiful terraces and decorated in yellow and green. It became the "in" nightclub on the sunny southern Florida coast. On Friday nights a television show was taped for viewing Sunday nights. The Lombardos were back as regulars on the television screen.

The 1964 governor's ball was held at the Port-O-Call, and Governor Bryant danced to "the sweetest music this side of heaven." The Sun Goddess Pageant, with its nineteen, white-gowned young ladies carrying bouquets of yellow roses was held at the Port-O-Call. A former Miss America, Miss Marilyn Van Derbur, announced the Sun Goddess and Mr. Sun to the strains of the Lombardo music.

But there were problems with this seemingly idealistic situation. "We'd leave there and come back to New York," Lebert says, "and the place would fold. So the next year before we left in the spring, we arranged for big stars like Liberace and Marlene Dietrich to keep the place rolling." The Lombardos were not making much profit as few homes were being sold. The prices were high for 1964 and cheaper developments, though perhaps not as fine as Tierra Verde, were springing up all over the coast. As well, the St. Petersburg area was characterized by many as a retirement area and young people simply didn't want to move there. Tierra Verde was also too quiet for many vacationers. "People would come for dinner and at ten o'clock you could shoot a cannon in the place and not hit anybody," one vacationer complained.

What complicated all this further was that the Belanti father and son were killed in an airplane crash in the Everglades. They were en route from New York to St. Petersburg in a small private plane piloted by Belanti Jr.

The Murchison brothers began to look for a buyer for Tierra Verde and the Lombardo band headed back to New York.

Tierra Verde had not been profitable for the Lombardo brothers. As they hadn't invested in it, however, they didn't actually lose any money. For the Royal Canadians, it was simply two sun-filled winters of fishing, boating and relaxing, while playing their music.

Freddie Kreitzer recalls wistfully, "That was going to be our winter home. The only reason it didn't work was because it was about six years ahead of its time. If it were now, it would be great."

6 On the Road

The Royal Canadians love a live audience. In other words, the single most important aspect of their music has always been "playing for happy people all the time," as Guy so often said. Playing over radio and appearing nightly at the Roosevelt Grill or Jones Beach was never enough for the Lombardo Brothers. They always felt, as did their happy fans, that it was important for the band to go on the road and see their audience in person.

By the early 1930s the Royal Canadians, and more particularly, the Lombardo brothers, had become stars of variety magazines, radio magazines, and local newspapers across North America. The Lombardo band was the cover story for magazines such as *Radio Stars* and *Radio Guide*. Pictures of Guy appeared everywhere, and *Radio Guide* even presented a giant head-to-waist gravure of Guy as their centerfold. Over the centerfold, which was printed with blue overtones in the style of the mid-thirties (making Guy, unfortunately, look slightly seasick), were the words: "With his three brothers [Victor had joined the band] and the kid next door, Guy Lombardo organized the Royal Canadians in 1918. Soft rhythms resulted when neighbors shouted, 'Quiet down!' But one day that subtle syncopation brought fame—made Guy the ace leader he is today!" The band members were not neglected. Newspapers grabbed every detail they could about the famous band. They told readers that Freddie once broke a finger and he nearly went frantic as he watched twenty-five substitute piano players try to take his

The Royal Canadians on Atlantic City's Steel Pier.

place, and that, for a good time, he took walks around Manhattan in the wee small hours. Derf Higman, one paper claimed, used to bet on horses, but his favorite diversion changed to buying meals for derelicts in New York's Bowery. The fans were told that Bern Davies' hobby was physics and that his guest room was decked out as a laboratory, and that George Gowans who was a pretty fair baseball player back in London now pitched pennies and studied aviation. Jeff Dillon was a star hockey player while Francis Henry earned his nickname Muff in school because the other boys remembered him missing a high fly in a baseball game, scoring a winning run for the school's opposition.

The Lombardo brothers have never disappointed their fans. Each year the Royal Canadians would take to the road. This is tough, grueling work, playing a different town every night, being sharp and musically awake. For the Royal Canadians, touring was a tonic, a fresh wind that sharpened and refined them. In the early days they were always impatient for the tour season to begin and joyful because every night brought a new and varied audience. Most of the members took to touring as a duck takes to water. For

3-25-30
PRESS

AMERICAN

The Royal Canadians were touring by plane as early as the 1930s.

Courtesy of Freddie Kreitzer

the original band members, small-town boys from London, it was a way to see North America.

"We were in the Roosevelt until late spring," Freddie remembers, "and then we'd go out for a couple of months."

When the band members were young, touring was not too much of a physical strain for them. "I didn't find it too bad," Freddie says, and George Gowans agrees. "You get used to it," he says musingly. Age has mellowed the memories. "I tell you one thing," Freddie continues. "As we got older it started to get draining."

The band members, of course, were separated from their wives and families when the band performed one-nighters. Freddie says his wife "never came with me unless we went to California or Las Vegas or some place where we'd stay five or six weeks."

Carmen's wife, Florence, used to fly to meet the band in later days in order to celebrate anniversaries, birthdays and other occasions. In the 1930s it was just too difficult to travel.

Bern Davies says, "In the early years, in the twenties, it was so bad and we drove by car. It could be raining like hell and there'd be mud right up to the runningboard. One night I was riding with the guitar player, Muff Henry, and he got a flat tire in the mud and so we picked everything out of the truck including his banjo and his guitar and laid it all behind the car to jack the car up and change the wheel. When the car dropped down off the jack it was probably in reverse; it backed up and ran over the guitar and the banjo!"

The Royal Canadians were one of the first bands to use airplanes to hop from town to town. At one stage they used small six-passenger Cessnas. The Royal Canadians approached their touring with the same pioneering spirit as their music. It is only fair to state, however, that the band could afford to take gambles such as using airplanes. They were popular, immensely popular, and the crowded dancehalls and the box office receipts made their ventures profitable and their gambles possible.

The band toured for financial reasons as well. Bern Davies says, "All the money is on the road. You can just break even in a hotel or supper room. You pay the band, take a couple of bucks for yourself and that's all. But on the road . . . if you can draw like we did . . ."

Guy always had a guaranteed advance of from $3,000 to $5,000 for one-nighters, and the crowds were usually so enormous the police and fire department used to come to maintain order and keep people off the bandstand.

In 1928 while playing at Toronto's Canadian National Exhibition, the Lombardo brothers met a young admirer who would grow

Courtesy of Alec Davidson

Nora and Alec Davidson with Guy Lombardo.

up to be one of their closest friends and fans. The boy, aged twelve, was Alec Davidson. "I guess they saw me so many times in front of that bandstand that finally, at the relief time, Larry Owen came down and he said, 'We always find you there in the crowd at the exhibition and you're so young. What is it?' I said, 'I guess I'm caught on this thing. I like it so much that I can't leave it alone. I'm here all the time.' "

Alec was an artist and later made special Christmas cards of the band and sent one to each member. He grew particularly close to Guy, Carmen, Lebert, Larry, and Derf.

Alec was the man who designed the crests on the bright red jackets that are still worn today. Until the end of World War II, the Royal Canadians wore blue jackets, short in the front and long in the back. There was no crest or distinctive Royal Canadian motif on them. "I heard them talking about a decent uniform. There was a guy on the dance floor wearing a red jacket, and I pointed and said, 'That looks like a Royal Canadian.' Kenny shouted, 'That's it! That's it!' I had a photograph of Guy that I had taken at the exhibition. I brought it home and airbrushed the red uniform on it and a crest I designed. I took it back to Guy, and that was it!" The crest, with its maple leaf background and crown reflecting the Canadian origin of the original band members, is made in Toronto every year.

Not one of the Royal Canadians is a Canadian citizen today. Each one in turn became an American after living there since 1923. The only Canadian Lombardo is Guy's sister Elaine. A few years ago, when crossing the Canadian border into Buffalo for a one-nighter, this gave rise to an amusing situation. A young Canadian customs officer, seeing the name Guy Lombardo's Royal Canadians on the bus, was systematically going through the bus asking every person his or her nationality. The only Canadians he could find, of course, were Elaine and a few Canadian friends Guy had brought along. The perplexed customs man asked, "Why do you call yourselves the Royal Canadians?" Guy serenely replied, "Oh well . . . If you don't know about it, it's a long story!"

No matter how busy the Lombardo brothers found themselves, they always had time for their hometown. In 1937 London, Ontario's Thames River overflowed its banks and almost half the town was under water. The brothers, hearing of the emergency, dropped everything else and telegrammed the mayor of London, offering to do benefit shows on behalf of victims of the flood. Naturally the offer was accepted. The brothers drove as close as they could to the city, trudging the last miles on foot through soggy mud and carrying their instruments by hand. City Councilor Mr. Norm Bradford, a childhood friend of Guy and Carmen, says, "There was a need here in their hometown and they came home to help it."

The Royal Canadians played London or Port Stanley, or both, every year on their spring and autumn tours. Every trip, the brothers would go sightseeing in London again, as if for the first time. Guy would rent a car, and any new members of the band were invited to come along to see where the brothers grew up, went to school, and first played. The brothers, in gratitude to the nuns who had taught them at St. Peter's Separate School, bought a statue of the Virgin Mary.

Hubert Lombardo, Guy's first cousin, a retired lithographer who has always lived in London and bears a striking resemblance to the bandleader, says that the brothers always came by to visit his mother, their Aunt Josie. "There was no high-hatting out of them. They were very sincere. They certainly tried to see all their old friends," he recalls. He also speaks of the high regard in which the brothers are held in London. "Whenever they were going to play Port Stanley or Centennial Hall or the University of Western Ontario, we could be sure that the phone would start ringing. We've had ladies call up who said they used to go out with Guy, all these stories . . . Some would be in tears."

In London's centennial year, 1955, the Lombardos came home to play a special concert. One Londoner, fan Mary Anne Campbell, who worked on the centennial committee, had a special present ready for Guy. It was a poem she composed herself which sums up the hometown feeling for Guy, his brothers and the London Royal Canadians. Here are three verses:

> The Lombardo boys left London,
> A very long time ago,
> And now they are back to liven up,
> Our hundredth birthday show.
>
> May we say down through the years, boys,
> As our pride in your band has grown,
> Sincerest thoughts and feelings,
> Were in our "Welcome Home."
>
> When at last you're gone once more boys,
> And this night fades to "way back when,"
> May your hearts be warmed by the joys you've brought,
> To your Old Home Town again.

Courtesy of Sue Fink

Don Byrnes, road
manager for the Royal
Canadians.

In the 1950s, the Royal Canadians started to travel almost exclusively by bus. Their yearly touring time was up to about four months a year. They have always rented their bus, and since 1959 their almost constant driver has been Don Byrnes. He was sent by his company, Walter Transit, out of New York City to pick up the band in Burlington, Ontario. A cheerful, efficient man, the Lombardos immediately liked Byrnes and his driving skill and requested him permanently. Before driving a bus Byrnes had led a very different life. "I grew up in Danbury, Connecticut, where they manufacture hats, and I was working in a hat shop before I started driving buses," he says. "The hat shops all went under. No one wears felt hats anymore; it's all cloth material. There are hardly any felt hats manufactured anymore." Working for Walters Transit, Byrnes drove all sorts of show-business groups before teaming up with the Royal Canadians. "I've taken out many Columbia Artists Productions. Years back I was with Lionel Hampton for a while." Over the twenty years Byrnes has been with the Royal

Courtesy of Lebert Lombardo

Guy on the road.

Canadians, his responsibilities have increased dramatically. Larry Owen, the sax player, had been road manager and music arranger for many years. After Larry had open heart surgery, Don did more of the road work and Owen worked in the office. When Owen retired, Don took over. Don says modestly, "I don't like to say that I'm the road manager. I've been doing it over the years and there's just no one else to do it."

Bill Richards and American Performing Arts have booked the band for over twenty years. Although it is true that in 1968 Guy also began to be booked by Associated Bookings and Columbia Artists Bookings, Richards still has booked them since Music Corporation of America days.

Richards makes the bookings and then passes a list of them on to Byrnes who sets up an itinerary and makes hotel reservations. Most of the jobs are repeated year after year. It's become an annual tradition in some towns to go see the Lombardos on this or that date.

The Lombardo bus has a sign saying Guy Lombardo in the front window and a fluorescent, red-painted sign that bears the words The Sweetest Music This Side of Heaven, surrounded by musical notes, on the back. It is an ordinary passenger bus except that some seats are turned so that the musicians can play cards, and there are racks in the back for the band members to hang up their garments. The brothers always sat at the front of the bus. Lebert occupied the single seat near the well and had a little table attached to the arm for his cigarettes and books.

Each musician receives a new Royal Canadian uniform each year and only carries one jacket with him as he travels. Jackets and pants are cleaned and pressed by motel and hotel valet services, but it is each musician's responsibility to see this is done. As most motels have coin laundries today, the musicians have no trouble doing their everyday wash-and-wear clothing. On top of their salary, each musician receives $154 a week expense money. Don Byrnes says, "Most of them double up in hotel rooms and save. The hotel situation is one of our worst enemies on the road. Very high. Every place you go is high today."

All the musicians are ready for the job an hour before the show, a tradition started many years ago. "They were never late for anything," Alec Davidson says. "They were always there an hour ahead. They couldn't relax in their rooms."

When the band played in one place for some time, Lebert's wife and children often came along. This led to complications over their schooling. Kenny tells the story: "When we went to Las Vegas and played the Desert Inn or Tropicana, because it was so pleasant and glamorous, he'd take the family. Well, Lizanne was school age so we had to get her into school somewhere. We went around and looked and we couldn't get her into any school." There were residency and taxation requirements that the Lombardos did not fulfill. "We went down to the Catholic school to see what we could do. Lo and behold, the Mother Superior was from London, Ontario! That's how we got her into school."

"They had a lot of fun on the road," Alec Davidson recalls. "I found later that the newer band members respected Guy in a different way because they didn't go to school with him and didn't grow up with him."

There were plenty of practical jokes among the band members. Someone, no one is sure who now, picked up an old wig and several of the boys decided Enemy, or Freddie, should wear it because he was getting a little thin on top. They'd take every chance to put it on his head and he'd toss it off. When the musicians were packing up after they'd finished the night's job, somebody would sneak the wig into his music case and the next night toss it onto Freddie's head again. Sometimes they even mailed the wig to destinations weeks ahead on their tour.

Courtesy of Kenny Gardner

While on tour in Texas, Carmen, Guy, and Lebert posed outside the first hotel to be owned by their friend, Conrad Hilton.

On one occasion the band was doing a live half-hour television special from the open-air deck of a beautiful country club. It began to rain, a driving forceful rain. The band was in a bandshell so they went on playing as if nothing had happened, but all the spectators and dancers ran for cover. One man stayed outside. He was very drunk and, without seeming to notice the change in the weather, began to drink all the unfinished drinks that were filling up with rainwater. The boys in the band, seeing him soaking wet, tried to stay serious and concentrate on their music, but it wasn't easy.

The original members did more touring as they got older, simply because the Royal Canadians spent fewer months at the Roosevelt Grill each year. According to Don Byrnes, from 1966 or 1967 on, the band played an average of thirty to thirty-one weeks of one-nighters a year. In 1978, when they did not play at Jones Beach, the band spent approximately forty-three weeks touring.

The band starts touring after New Year's Eve with a January and February tour of Florida. From there they continue north through Louisiana and Arkansas, the Southwest and Midwest. By spring they are in eastern Canada and the northeastern United States. In the past the band then played at Jones Beach, now they simply spend a little more time on each leg of their tour all through the year. By autumn they are back in Canada and from there they drive south to the northwestern and southwestern United States.

In the fall of 1978, the Royal Canadians, led by Lebert's son Bill (see Chapter 14), played for a successful week-long cruise to the Bahamas aboard the *S.S. Rotterdam*. "It was an absolutely beautiful boat," Bill says. "It's the flagship of the Holland American Cruise Lines and displaces 38,000 gross tons. There were 1,100 passengers. It has indoor and outdoor pools. It also has a beautiful theater where we played. We played one black-tie party on board, the rest were suit and tie. The people just loved it. There were a lot of older people there, but some younger ones as well. It went over really well." The Royal Canadians played every other night. As well, rock groups, a Filippino group, and other entertainment was featured on the boat.

The band then went on to the Holliday House in Pittsburgh. "We just followed Phyllis Diller there. She was in for a month," Don Byrnes says. The Holliday House is a dinner-show room and so the band plays two shows a night, a "cocktail" show and a midnight show.

Guy Lombardo's Royal Canadians are performing the same function they did sixty years ago and more, and that is making people happy!

7 No Business Like Show Business

During their long years in the spotlight, the Lombardo brothers were the friends of many show-business personalities.

When the boys temporarily left the Roosevelt Grill for the 1933 to 1935 winter seasons, they played at the Coconut Grove in Los Angeles. Here they met and grew friendly with people they had formerly only seen on the screen, people like Louis B. Mayer, Jeanette MacDonald, Errol Flynn, Ginger Rogers, Loretta Young, Ronald Colman, and Joan Crawford.

Lebert remembers, "I knew Carole Lombard very well. She was a wonderful person. You see, years ago when we were in California, we'd be at the Coconut Grove for a couple of months so I'd rent a home. The last one I rented was John Monsider's and it was back to back with Carole Lombard's home. Now, my first wife's name was Carol. Carole Lombard was an awful kidder; she was always playing gags. One day we heard a rap on the door and it was Carole and her secretary Madelaine Fields who used to be a star in the Mack Sennett comedies when Carole Lombard was a student, just a no-account. Madelaine used to give her stockings and clothes. Later the situation reversed. When Carole became a star, she made Madelaine her secretary. So the two of them are at the door. Now Carole Lombard liked to swear—you'd see this innocent-looking face—but swear! Well, she started laying into me and my wife, Carol. 'What do you mean, our mail is getting mixed up! How dare you call yourself Carol Lombardo?' It was just a gag, but after that we became very good friends."

Other close California friends of Lebert's were Alan and Sue Carol Ladd. Lebert had known Sue Carol before her marriage to Ladd. "I'd known her for many, many years when she was married to Nick Stuart. He was a bandleader. You see, they used to have screen tests and Sue Carol won a chance to take one. So did Nick Stuart. When they went to California they teamed the two of them up. They made a lot of pictures together. Then later on there were mother-in-law problems. When talkies came in, Sue Carol couldn't appear in pictures because she had a bad lisp, and the mother was blaming Nick for Sue not making a go at talkies. So they were finally divorced.

A promotion shot from the thirties.

Courtesy of MCA

Guy, Carmen, Lebert, and Victor Lombardo.

"Nick and Sue had two girls. We were in Colorado Springs a few months ago and who came backstage to see me? Carol Lee! That was quite a thrill because I haven't seen her for years. She's now married to an executive at Paramount Pictures."

The Lombardo band tried to get the popular actress and singer Cheryl Ladd for the 1979 New Year's Eve program. Kenny says, "We wanted Cheryl Ladd of *Charlie's Angels* because there's more or less a family connection. We have long known Alan Ladd's family. Alan Ladd's son is Cheryl Ladd's husband. Either the Ladd family is in the Lombardo family or the Lombardo family is in the Ladd family. We never went to California without spending time with Alan and Sue Carol, and whenever they came east they spent their time with us too."

Cheryl was unable to appear on the show. Kenny explains, "There's something we don't understand about that particular business that she is in. When they make serials there is an automatic hiatus over the New Year's period. Usually they make prior commitments to do a movie or something else during that period. And that's what she's doing. We heard her sing and we said, 'Hey, do you want to be on the New Year's Eve show?' And, whammo! That's when she found out she was engaged to do something else. It's even out of the country, I believe.''

The Royal Canadians have been associated with three movies. The earliest, *Many Happy Returns*, was made for Paramount Pictures and released in 1934. It was filmed during the band's stay in California and directed by Norman McLeod. Its stars were Ray Milland, George Burns, and Gracie Allen, and the dancers Veloz and Yolanda. The band appeared on screen and Guy and Lebert had speaking roles. Also appearing in the movie were Larry Adler, the harmonica player, and tap-dancers Rutledge and Taylor. Among the songs featured in this movie were Carmen's composition "The Sweetest Music This Side of Heaven" and "Auld Lang Syne."

Kenny Gardner had not yet joined the band but he came to know George Burns and Gracie Allen some years later. He remembers, "George and Gracie actually started on radio with the boys. Gracie was very astute. Don't let anybody kid you that she was as she acted. She was a very astute showman." Kenny says that Burns is definitely as relaxed as he appears, "just through the fact he's been around so long that he knows what he's doing."

Lebert remembers young Shirley Temple. "She was on the same set when we made that Paramount picture. She was doing *Little Miss Marker* with Adolph Menjou. Did you ever see that? It was a great picture! Mae West was also making a picture. Oh golly, there were seven or eight pictures being made at the same time!"

Another movie in which the band made an appearance was *No Leave, No Love*, filmed in 1945 and released in 1946. The stars in this slow-moving MGM production were the young Van Johnson, Keenan Wynn, and singer Patricia Kirkwood, all talented professionals in their fields. However, there wasn't much they could do to salvage a script hastily changed due to the abrupt end of the war. "It was fun," George Gowans laughs. "It started out as a war picture, but then the Japanese war was over so they had to change it around, front and back."

Guy was extremely annoyed about the making of this picture. The Royal Canadians appeared for rehearsal only to find themselves surrounded by the MGM Symphony Orchestra.

The band's music was a part of one other movie in which they did not appear. United Artists' *Stage Door Canteen* was one of the ten most popular movies of 1943 with cameo appearances by Katherine Hepburn, Harpo Marx, William Demarest, George

Raft, Ray Bolger, Paul Muni, Merle Oberon, Helen Hayes, Edgar Bergen and Charlie McCarthy, and, of course, music by Guy Lombardo's Royal Canadians. "In the other two movies they participated in the story itself," Dave Kressley, an ardent Royal Canadians' fan says. "In this movie they just filmed a few tunes that were going to be used in it. They didn't do any acting. Actually they ended up using only one song which was called 'Sleep, Baby, Sleep in Your Jeep.'"Sister Rosemarie sang the vocal in the movie.

Five other famous bands were heard in *Stage Door Canteen*: Kay Kyser, Benny Goodman, Freddy Martin, Xavier Cugat, and Count Basie.

At the Roosevelt Grill, the Pavillon on Long Beach, Long Island, and the Starlight Room of the Waldorf-Astoria where the band played during the summer, the brothers had a following that included men such as Woodsworth Donahue, Dan Topping, Walter Chrysler Jr., and T. H. Daugherty, president of the Metropolitan Life Insurance Company. Celebrities came to see and be seen. Also, untried performers often got their first break in Long Beach's Pavillon. On any night, names such as Flo Ziegfield, Ethel Merman, George M. Cohan, Ethel Shutta, and George Olson could be seen.

Courtesy of Saul Richman

The Lombardo band in the early 1930s.

Lebert remembers the time vividly and tells stories of his friends. "Bill Paley, the owner of CBS, used to come down to the Roosevelt and help us get the band balanced. He was a good friend of ours." In those early days, even the president of a radio network came out from behind his desk.

Kenny remembers Bing Crosby well. "Bing represented, when he was in New York in the early thirties, shall we say a younger generation, and at first it was rather critical of the Lombardo music. Later on he recognized the strength of the Lombardo music and the Lombardo status. We spent an evening together when we played West Palm Beach, and Bing came over and was backstage all night long. We had a lot of talk.

"On another occasion shortly before he died, Bing was in the city with Dixie, his first wife. Bing and Guy had a mutual friend, a very highly thought of music publisher, Rocco Bacco, and Rocco brought Dixie to the Waldorf. In the course of the evening Rocco, Bing, and later Lebe all sat around, and all they talked about was music. Dixie saw me sitting on the bandstand and hollered for me to come down. So I came down and sat at the table." Presumably Dixie had heard enough music talk for one evening.

Lebert reveals that Jack Benny, the brothers' close friend, had a touch of hard times every so often as do all show-business people. "I'll never forget the time we were at the Chicago Theater and Jack Benny, this was in radio days, came up to Guy's dressing room. He was almost in tears. He said, 'Why isn't there something for me on radio?' and Guy said, 'Well, Jack, things will develop . . .' And then sure enough, a year or two later he got on that Jello program."

In 1949, the brothers decided to open a restaurant. Close by Guy's Long Island home, at the foot of South Grove Street, was an established seafood restaurant named John Liota's East Point House. Liota was contemplating getting out of the business and so he sold the rights to the restaurant to the brothers. The land on which the restaurant stood jutted into a lovely bay. It was owned by the town of Hempstead, Long Island.

Brother Joe was called in to give his expert opinion regarding expansion and renovation. When Joe stated that the rooms could not be reconstructed because the restaurant was built on marshland, the brothers asked him to design a new restaurant.

Joe designed a restaurant which looked like a ship. It had three dining decks where patrons could overlook the water, and later an upstairs room was converted into a catering hall that could seat 700. Outside the restaurant, sunk in the water, were striped poles at which passing boatmen could dock their boats in order to go into the restaurant to dine. Guy's wife, Lilliebell, decorated the restaurant on a nautical theme. Many of Guy's racing trophies were put on display. It was managed by Lilliebell's sister's husband, Bill Frey, a man who had considerable experience running restaurants in Cleveland. Guy particularly recommended Canadian pea soup and Canadian Labatt's Pale India Ale to his customers. The restaurant, which boasted "the sweetest lobsters this side of heaven," did extremely good business during the summer months.

The brothers offered their patrons "nightly dancing on the deck," and when it could be managed, the Royal Canadians themselves played at the restaurant. After the Lombardos had operated the Jones Beach Marine Theatre for several years, they offered a package including a dinner, ferry ride and admission to the theater. It was a great success.

Guy Lombardo's East Point House became a gathering spot for show-business people out to enjoy a leisurely evening meal. Patrons such as Perry Como, Freddy Martin, Stitch Henderson, Fay Emerson, Phil Harris, Alice Faye, and Tommy Dorsey would drive out to Long Island to eat and chat with their friend Guy Lombardo.

After Bill Frey died, the management of the restaurant became more and more of a problem. The brothers leased the restaurant to others and at one point sold part of their share in it. Still, they would often be called when on tour about this or that problem in connection with the restaurant.

By the early seventies, the restaurant was closed and shuttered. Lebert explains what happened next. "All of a sudden one of our local politicians got us to open the restaurant in partnership with Karl Hoppl's Catering. He has two or three big catering places on the island. So we all went over to the township office at Hempstead. We had our lawyers and they had theirs. Karl Hoppl was going to build another place in conjunction with ours. Then we took off our insurance and Hoppl was supposed to put his on. A couple of months later the place burnt down and he didn't have it insured. We lost everything, all Guy's trophies from his speedboat racing, all our kitchen equipment, everything." That ended the restaurant career of Guy Lombardo.

Guy and his brothers have helped a lot of other musicians to get their start in show business. In fact, one summer Guy suggested a young bandleader whose style he respected and thought innovative to be the band's replacement at the Roosevelt Grill for a couple of months. The young man was Lawrence Welk!

Guy also discovered the talented trumpet player and swing bandleader, Louis Prima, while the brothers were on a trip to New

Louis Armstrong with Guy Lombardo on stage at Jones Beach Marine Theatre (see Chapter 9) in 1966. The young man in the white blazer is Joel Grey.

Orleans in 1934. Guy brought Prima and his four-man band to New York and soon Prima was the sensational headliner at a Fifty-second Street club, the Famous Door. From there, the street became known as Swing Street as jazz and swing clubs opened one after another.

Alec Davidson remembers how Guy helped many others get their break. "When you think of the Mills Brothers," he says, "it was Guy who was instrumental in getting them on the air. He had heard them in the South, but in those days because of their color they didn't get a chance. It was Guy who went to CBS and told them about this dandy group. They got a regular fifteen-minute show. When the Lombardos met the Mills Brothers at the Royal York Hotel in Toronto one night when Guy had just finished at the bandstand at Ontario Place, I was really touched to see people that appreciated each other so much!"

For many years the Lombardos mounted extravagant musical productions at the Jones Beach Marine Theatre (see Chapter 9) and were able to present many established stars to a new public. As well, they were able to offer a showcase of new talent. Actors and actresses such as Lauritz Melchior, Gene Nelson, Andy Devine, Dom DeLuise, Fritz Weaver, Arthur Treacher, Constance Towers, Bonnie Franklin, Christopher Ewett, and Robert Clary have all appeared on the Jones Beach stage.

In 1966 a young actor named Joel Grey appeared in the Jones Beach production of *Mardi Gras*. Kenny remembers, "Joel Grey personally did such a fine job out at Jones Beach that they actually wrote a part for him in the New York stage show *Cabaret*. And so in 1967 when the Lombardo brothers tried to get Grey for their production *Arabian Nights*, Grey had to politely refuse them."

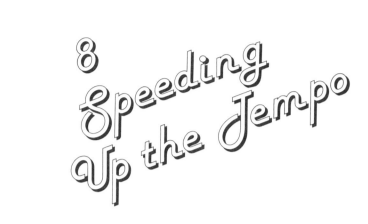

8 Speeding Up the Tempo

Speedboat racing, or powerboat racing as it is called today, is a dangerous sport. It requires guts, determination, and courage. This is the sport that Guy Lombardo decided to enter in 1939.

He had been familiar with powerboats ever since Papa bought a small one when Guy was a boy and raced up and down the Thames River on Sunday afternoons. Papa would hit speeds of seven or eight miles an hour.

Guy loved the water and he loved boats. In the late 1920s he bought a small runabout that could go up to thirty-five miles an hour. A couple of years later he traded up to a boat that reached forty miles an hour. He used them for exploring the bays and inlets of Long Island.

After the stock market crash Guy bought a fifty-five-foot yacht that he and his wife used as a summer home. The teak and mahogany yacht came from a shipbuilder who had been left with it after the man who originally ordered it lost his money in the crash. It had sleeping quarters for six with accommodation for a crew. Guy called the beautiful boat *Tempo*. Every boat he bought from that time on would be named *Tempo* as well.

The boat became a refuge for Guy from the hectic music business in New York City. And so in 1939 Guy bought property on South Grove Street, Freeport, Long Island and bulkheaded the property (built a mooring), giving him a private place to dock his boat. Fans, however, got into the habit of mooring their boats near Guy in

Courtesy of Alec Davidson

The chance of a glimpse of Guy in *Tempo* was one of the attractions at the East Point House restaurant.

public docks and inviting themselves aboard *Tempo* for a drink and an autograph. Guy never had the heart to turn his fans away. A year later, Guy and Lilliebell built a home on the South Grove property. Mrs. Lombardo still lives there.

On a visit to Toronto in 1939, Guy saw one of the newly designed hydroplane racing boats. These boats are built with projections from the forward section of the hull—the projections are called sponsons—and at high speeds only the sponsons and the propeller at the stern are in contact with the water. This causes the boat to ride above the water—to plane—and increases potential speed by reducing the drag caused by the hull plowing through the water. One famous Canadian boat, *Miss Supertest III*, at a speed of one hundred miles an hour, had only two square feet of its hull in contact with the water.

Guy bought a hydroplane with an engine capacity of 225 cubic inches that could reach a speed of eighty miles an hour. With this purchase he entered the world of speedboat racing. He was thirty-eight years old. In a dangerous sport in which accidents are frequent and fatalities not rare, Guy was trusting that his reflexes were quick, as quick as many of his young competitors. The Lombardo family was proud of Guy's courage and ambition, but tried to discourage his interest in the sport. They feared for his life and also that his new interest would conflict with his leadership of the Royal Canadians. It didn't. Music, although often by a slim margin, always came before speedboat racing.

Courtesy of the Champion Spark Plug Company

Mr. Jim Thompson of London, Ontario, owner and designer of the Rolls Royce-airplane-engined *Miss Supertest III*, winner of the Harmsworth Trophy (the world's speedboat championship) in 1959 and twice its successful defender, says of speedboat racing, "It certainly is dangerous. The water is never the same. It is not like a road; a road doesn't change under you. Every time the driver goes around the circuit, it will be different."

In hydroplane racing the circuit is usually an oval shape and is usually one and two-thirds miles in length. A racer usually drives three laps or five miles which enables him to set a five-mile speed or lap record. Although every race is not set out this way, this is the time and distance suggested by l'Union Internationale Motonautique, based in Brussels. This coordinating body is the parent of the North American organizations, the American Power Boat Association, the Canadian Boating Federation, and the Federation Mexicana Motonautique.

Each race consists of two heats. Vic Waring, executive director of the Canadian Boating Federation, explains, "You get points for your position in each heat. Someone could come up first in the first heat and third in the second heat and still be winner of the race. He'd get 400 points for his first and 225 points for his third place, making 625. If another driver got two seconds at 300 points each, ending up with 600, the man with the first and third would win."

Each heat lasts only three to four minutes in the big hydroplane races. The boats that were being raced in the forties and fifties would reach speeds of 150 miles an hour.

Guy began racing his 225-cubic-inch hydroplane in 1940. In his first race he missed the start because the roar of all the boats around him drowned the noise of the gun. Later he learned to look for the blue smoke of the starting gun.

In 1942 he bought a second 225-cubic-inch boat which he again named *Tempo*. Vic Waring says, "He was the kind who wanted to be on top, and as innovations came in he would be the first person to have them built into his boat." That year Guy entered twenty-two races and won twenty-one of them!

For the rest of World War II, speedboat racing stopped completely. After the war, the sport began again but with a difference. Hundreds of war-surplus airplane engines were for sale and racers began to install them in their boats. The mechanics, however, did not have the plastics and alloys that have since become available because of advances made in space technology. Some of the boats disintegrated at high speeds because of heat or vibration. Vic Waring says, "They were developing the sport from scratch. They were using flexible couplings that were probably meant for tractors."

In speedboat racing there are many events, classified by engine size, ranging from 225 cubic inches to unlimited. In the unlimited class, engines can be as large as the owner wants, but the boat itself must not be more than forty feet long.

Each year drivers compete to win the Triple Crown in three races: the Red Bank Sweepstakes in New Jersey, the President's Cup in Washington, and the Gold Cup. The Gold Cup race is held either in Detroit or at a location chosen by the winner of the cup the year before.

In 1946, Guy entered his new boat in the Triple Crown. *Tempo VI* was a 450-horsepower boat formerly called *My Sin* by its previous owner, Zammie Simmons of the mattress building family.

Guy had reservations about the Gold Cup, held that year in Detroit. Speedboat racing had become a rich man's sport. Only very large boats were allowed to compete for the Gold Cup and Guy considered this unfair. He suggested that the race be open to boats large and small, down to the 225-cubic-inch size. He said that the small boats might stand a chance of winning if the larger boats developed problems. The officials of the race agreed.

That year Guy won the Red Bank Sweepstakes and the Gold Cup. He lost the President's Cup, outrun by a boat of 1,500 horsepower.

The next year, 1947, Guy chose the site of the Gold Cup race. With the aid of the U.S. Coast Guard he picked Jacob Riis Park on Long Island. On the day of the race a combination of floating debris, rain, and trouble with *Tempo*'s lubrication system caused him to lose the race.

In 1948, in the Gold Cup in Detroit, Guy had a serious accident that almost cost him his life. With Guy racing at 125 miles an hour, the rudder and propeller of the boat in front of him failed. He had three choices: he could crash into the boat that was ahead of him and probably kill the driver; he could veer into a pier jutting into the river and perhaps kill many spectators; or he could spin his wheel, shut off his engine, and go into a broadsiding stall. Guy chose the third. The boat overturned and Guy hit the water. He was knocked unconscious and broke his arm. When he came to, he went to the hospital, had the arm set, and returned to the race. He kept moving about all day, ignoring the doctor's warnings that he was in shock. Later that night he flew home to Freeport. It was not until he woke up the next day that he realized that he had had an accident. Nature's shock absorbers had kept him unaware of just how close he had come to death.

Guy had been thrown from the boat and that was what saved his life. Speedboat drivers do not wear seatbelts. Vic Waring says, "A boat will do one of three things. It will barrel-roll sideways, it will barrel-roll forward, or it will lose a sponson and just flip over. If drivers were tied in their boats, we'd have a lot of deaths." Today's drivers often have parachutes. If the boat goes over, the driver ejects himself up and out of the boat.

Guy conducts the band from *Tempo* at Jones Beach Marine Theatre.

Guy continued racing until 1954, the year he and his brothers began to produce the musical extravaganzas at Jones Beach Marine Theatre. Guy no longer had time to spend his summers speedboat racing. He continued to fight for safety regulations in the sport. Often he acted as an official starter for races of all types for the American Powerboat Racing Association and the Canadian Boating Federation. When the Royal Canadians played at Tierra Verde, Florida, in the mid-sixties, Guy raced 225s in the area.

The *Tempo* in which he won the Gold Cup in 1946 is in a speed museum in Daytona Beach, Florida. His last boat, *Tempo VII*, has recently been given to a museum in Atlantic City.

Guy took his speedboating seriously. It was not, as some critics have claimed, a stunt to publicize the Royal Canadians. After all, Guy not only owned the boats, he drove them himself. Jim Thompson says, "He was a good driver, no doubt about it. He was a very capable driver." Vic Waring agrees. "He became a véry skilled driver. You can't get into one of those boats and stay in the company he was in and do as well as he did without being able to drive."

9 Sound Studio to Beach Theater

As the bands got bigger in the thirties, so did the audiences, and so did the business of running the bands. Radio, movies, vaudeville, and touring brought millions of new fans, and there was a lot of money to be made. A fair-sized dance band needs an army of people as its support staff: managers, arrangers, publicists, stage directors, maintenance men, and office staff. In the case of some bands, the artists themselves ran the business, dealt with the receipts and bookings, and handled the practical details.

One of the big business concerns of the thirties grew out of Fred Waring's orchestra, the Pennsylvanians. By 1936, his outfit's headquarters occupied an entire floor of an office building on Broadway and employed dozens of people. The popular Casa Loma orchestra was run as a corporation with each member of the band owning a share of the business. Founded in Detroit by musicians who had worked together in Jean Goldkette's orchestra, the members decided to stay together after Goldkette dissolved the band, and the men held regular business meetings, declared dividends and elected officers once a year. Glen Gray who was often called leader of the band because he was president of the corporation for some time, did not hold the baton but played saxophone.

The Royal Canadians, on the other hand, have always been owned by the three original Lombardo brothers, Guy, Carmen, and Lebert. As mentioned earlier, they became clients of the Music Corporation of America and brothers Jules and Billy Stein when they moved to Chicago in 1927. By the mid-thirties, MCA took care of the business dealings, promotions and problems of 110 dance bands, including those directed by Wayne King, Ben Bernie, Gus Arnheim, Eddy Duchin, and Kay Kyser. They managed more bands than any other agency. With an agent that took care of everything from contracts and proper staging to their investments, the Lombardo brothers were free to devote themselves to their music. In 1936, while Waring, Rudy Vallee, Whiteman, and others had huge operating expenses, Guy had only two permanent staff members, his secretary, Miss Viola Nugent, and Boyd Bunch, the band's arranger.

The Lombardo music company, Olman Publishing, was formed in the late thirties. Sister Elaine was secretary and the office was run by Miss Ruth Andres, affectionately called Miss Connie, who still works for the Lombardo band. After a few years in a business, the Lombardos, never good businessmen, sold their company as a tax write-off in 1943. Shortly after the sale, a record they produced became a best seller. It was "Heartache," with lyrics by Sammy Cahn and played by Ted Weem's orchestra. According to Guy, the company had been sold for less than $8,000. If they had not sold it, Weem's record would have made them a small fortune. Incidentally, Cahn had written another big hit, "Rhythm Is Our Business."

The Royal Canadians stayed with MCA through its spectacular growth. Jules and Bill Stein are now the owners of Universal Productions, the movie company, and Decca Records. Kenny Gardner explains: "MCA was started by Dr. Jules Stein during the days in Chicago. They expanded it into a nationwide corporation as a booking agency. They signed up talent. Then they branched into production which hired their talent and produced radio, television, and Broadway plays. Then the U.S. government stepped in and said, 'Wait a minute. You can't have control of both artists and production.' So MCA then decided to forgo the booking agency."

But by this time the bands were a very small part of MCA's business. As Elaine realistically says, "In the fifties, the big bands started to peter out."

Kenny continues, "When Lou Wasserman of MCA saw the coming of TV he decided to dissolve the booking department and move the company to California. He bought Universal Studios, which was at that time a class B operation, not like MGM or Twentieth Century-Fox. So the fellows who had worked in the booking agency scattered to the four winds and built their own smaller corporations."

One of these bookers was Bill Richards. He now owns the Agency of the Performing Arts in Chicago and has been the Royal Canadians' main booker since the early sixties.

The Royal Canadians recorded their first two records that were released in 1924. The record business was very new and the Lombardos have always been proud of having been in at the beginning, way before their friends Bing Crosby and Rudy Vallee. The recordings were issued by the Gennett label in Indianapolis, and the nine original Royal Canadians—Guy, Carmen, Lebert, Freddie Kreitzer, George Gowans, Derf Higman, Jeff Dillon, Muff Henry, and Eddie Mashurette—and the two who had joined in Cleveland —Larry Owen from that city and Bern Davies from London—laid down in wax the tone and style that would be so widely loved and imitated. Of course, the band was raw at this stage and the five songs recorded then ("Cy" and "So This Is Venice" on one disk and "Mama's Gone Good-bye" and "Cottonpickers' Ball" on the other) were never hits except much later with collectors of Lombardo memorabilia. According to Dave Kressley, a Lombardo fan, they had first recorded "Someone Loves You After All" but it was never issued. Since then they have recorded for Columbia while in Cleveland, Decca Records, then owned by their friend Jack Knapp (who had worked with the Brunswick Record Company), Victor Records and Capitol.

In 1934 Decca released four Lombardo records ("Love in Bloom/Down by the Old Mill Stream"; "Moonglow/Blue in Love"; "Give Me a Heart to Sing to/Stars Fell on Alabama"; "I Saw Stars/Have a Little Dream on Me"), all now treasured collectors' items. The Lombardos were recording stars.

The Royal Canadians' market was worldwide. Guy once said, "Our biggest record markets outside the United States are the Philippines, Australia, and Japan." He added, "One of our TV series was the number one show in Australia for years."

Lebert says, "One year after World War II we sold eleven million records of all different albums."

Lebert claims that the profits from these eleven million records were all put into one of the Lombardo brothers' pet projects, the musical extravaganzas they produced at Jones Beach Marine Theatre on Long Island.

Jones Beach State Park was built under the auspices of Robert Moses, the master builder and planner responsible for bridges, parks, and housing projects in New York City. It opened in 1929 and the Jones Beach Stadium, as the marine theater was originally called, followed a few years later. A wooden structure with seats for 10,000 people faced a stage which sat in a lagoon in front of

Courtesy of the Long Island State Park and Recreation Commission

The Marine Theatre in Jones Beach State Park photographed from the air.

Zach's Bay. Tryouts for Olympic water events were held here as well as such events as the *Daily News* Water Derby. Operettas, including such famous ones as *Firefly, Bittersweet, Rose Marie*, and musical comedies such as *Sally, Irene, and Mary, Of Thee I Sing, Anything Goes*, and *Roberta*, were produced on the floating stage. Even grand opera was presented: *La Traviata, Aida*, and *Pagliacci*.

During the war years the operation was suspended; however, near the end of the war the old wooden stadium was dismantled and hurried construction began. Out of this emerged an 8,200-seat concrete stadium on shore with a larger, floating stage. In 1952 and 1953, Mike Todd, Jr., the lovely Elizabeth Taylor on his arm, put on a musical show entitled *A Night in Venice*. It was not profitable, and Robert Moses, president of the Long Island State Park Commission, and Sid Shapiro, Chief Engineer and General Manager of the commission, agreed to try to persuade Guy Lombardo to produce the extravaganzas.

Guy never could resist a challenge, and what he was being offered here involved his two greatest loves, music and water. In 1954 Guy, Carmen, and Lebert produced their first show at Jones Beach.

During the first two years the brothers produced the shows, the financial risks were borne entirely by the Lombardos. The first, *Arabian Nights*, was written by Carmen and his partner John Jacob Loeb. George Marion Jr. wrote the adaptation for the play. The Lombardos chose well in Marion, a man of excellent reputation and great experience.

Starting out as a creator of humorous titles for silent movies, Marion had worked on such films as *The Gay Divorcee* for Fred Astaire and Ginger Rogers, *You Can't Cheat an Honest Man* with W. C. Fields, *Love Me Tonight* with Maurice Chevalier, and *The Big Broadcast* with Bing Crosby. Marion had worked on stage plays before coming to Jones Beach. He had written the books and lyrics for such Broadway shows as *Early to Bed*, *Marinka*, *Beat the Band*, *Allah Be Praised*, *The Gypsy Baron*, and *Toplitzsky of Notre Dame*.

The Arabian Nights tales of Sinbad the Sailor and Aladdin and his magic lamp, tales almost a thousand years old, are able to charm any audience, and this was certainly the case the first year of the Lombardo productions. Lauritz Melchior, the operatic star, played the sultan. Another audience delight was S. S. Polky, a blue canvas whale with white polka dots that sailed on a barge. He was written into the story to carry shipwrecked Sinbad and his sailors. Polky sported a gold bicuspid and spouted water all over the sailors. Later, when the brothers repeated *Arabian Nights* in 1967, Polky was eighty feet long and was powered by four forty-mile-per-hour outboard engines. His rib cage was like the structure of an ocean liner with styrofoam sheathing glued to the frames bolted to the ribbing. Even with Polky's enormous size it took set designer Peter Dohanos only two weeks to build him; Dohanos had carved a miniature Polky to scale as a model. Polky Jr. was thirty-six inches long and Dohanos used a bread knife to cut the styrofoam when carving him.

After all expenses, the 1954 production profits were twenty-six dollars, thirteen for the brothers and thirteen for the state. The next year, a summer of hurricanes, the brothers lost $300,000 and vowed to quit being extravaganza producers. But Robert Moses liked the Lombardo touch; from that time on New York State advanced $250,000 for production money, money the brothers would pay back only if they made a profit. For the production expenses above that amount, the Lombardos would have to gamble their own money. The brothers talked to Moses and agreed to come back to Jones Beach.

Of course, every show produced by the Lombardo brothers over their twenty-four year association cannot be described in detail. There were just too many:

1954-55	*Arabian Nights*
1956-57	*Show Boat*
1958-59	*Song of Norway*
1960	*Hit the Deck*
1961-62	*Paradise Island*
1963-64	*Around the World in 80 Days*
1965-66	*Mardi Gras*
1967	*Arabian Nights*
1968-69	*South Pacific*
1970-71	*The Sound of Music*
1972	*The King and I*
1973	*Carousel*
1974	*Fiddler on the Roof*
1975	*Oklahoma*
1976	*Show Boat*
1977	*Finian's Rainbow*

It's easy to see from this list that the brothers chose plays that gave them a chance to exploit their waterfront setting and lagoon-encircled stage. The plays themselves were drawn from all quarters. Carmen Lombardo and John Jacob Loeb wrote *Arabian Nights*, *Paradise Island*, which coincided with the celebration of statehood for Hawaii, and *Mardi Gras*, which has legends and tales of New Orleans complete with a pirate ship. *Around the World in 80 Days* was adapted from the Mike Todd movie, and *Hit the Deck* was a new production of *Shore Leave* which had played at the Belasco Theatre in New York for 352 performances in 1927. It was written by composer Vincent Youmans, scriptwriter Herbert Fields, and lyricists Les Robin and Clifford Grey. In *Hit the Deck* the writer for Jones Beach invented a new character: Guy Lombardo, played by Guy Lombardo.

There were free programs for each play and, for a price, beautifully illustrated souvenir booklets that not only told the history of the play and life stories of the actors, but also gave pictures and stories of Guy Lombardo's Royal Canadians. Some years there were articles about Guy's boat racing, which was not unreasonable considering the theater's water location.

Theatergoers could enjoy the attractions of Jones Beach State

Courtesy of the Long Island State Park and Recreation Commission
A scene from *Mardi Gras*, at Jones Beach, 1965.

Park and see a play all in one day. Alec Davidson says, "The beach itself is one of the world's great beaches, white sand and so orderly. When you went through the tollgates into the beach area, the guards would watch and if they saw anything that looked as if it might present problems they'd phone other guards and let them know to watch for car license number so and so. And if the people weren't behaving, the police just asked them to leave and gave them their money back so nobody would be disturbed. You could walk for miles and everything was in order." Visitors could swim, cycle, dine, and then see Guy Lombardo's production. Many New Yorkers viewed a trip to Jones Beach as a miniholiday.

For the Lombardos it was also a chance to spend the summer at home on Long Island with their families. None of the brothers lived more than a forty-minute drive away from the park. As for the band members, in the early days of Jones Beach most of the members were originals or longtimers with the band, and they mostly lived in New York City. Summers of staying put at Jones Beach meant less road touring for all concerned, and by 1954 this was perhaps most welcome. The band members were in their fifties and wanted to settle down a bit more.

During the first few years the pit orchestra was the fifteen Royal

Canadians with recruits from the New York area. In a few shows such as *Hit the Deck* and *Mardi Gras*, the band actually played onstage. Later the pit orchestra, which numbered thirty to forty players changed in composition. Kenny explains, "Originally all of us were from New York City and had homes here. But then through natural attrition, some of the boys retiring, we got musicians from elsewhere. Well, it would hardly be feasible to have these boys come down here and only play for an hour a night so these boys, if they wished, played in the pit orchestra as well as onstage."

The play, *Mardi Gras*, was presented in 1965 and starred David Atkinson, Ralph Purdom, Karen Shepard, and Wilbur de Paris and his New Orleans Jazz. The following year this successful play was repeated with Atkinson, Purdom, and Shepard. However, the dixieland music was played by Louis Armstrong and his All Stars. This was a chance for Louis and the Lombardo brothers, lifelong friends to work together once more.

How *Mardi Gras* was conceived, developed, and reached the stage is a good example of the way all the plays were handled. After the opening of *Around the World in 80 Days*, the writer of the play,

Courtesy of the Long Island State Park and Recreation Commission

Louis Armstrong (center) plays on stage in the Jones Beach production of *Mardi Gras* in 1966.

100

The 1963 production at Jones Beach Marine Theatre was *Around the World in 80 Days*.

Courtesy of the Long Island State Park and Recreation Commission

Sig Herzig, was visited by Guy, Carmen, Lebert, and Arnold Spector, the managing director for the Lombardos of all the Jones Beach productions. They were so happy with *Around the World* they invited him to write the play for the next year. Looking out at the crescent-shaped stage set on the water, Guy suggested New Orleans as a setting. Herzig suggested the New Orleans' Mardi Gras as the theme. You could almost hear Carmen's and Johnny Loeb's minds clicking and soon Johnny was humming bars from songs that would later be in the show.

By autumn Guy and Carmen were on the road touring, and the phone company made a fortune as Lombardo-Loeb-Herzig calls flew fast and furious. The state park commissioners attended a run-through in December, loved the show, and gave it approval to open in July.

Courtesy of the Long Island State Park and Recreation Commission
Guy conducts for dancers in the dancing tent at Jones Beach Marine Theatre in 1968.

This particular play is a lovely, romantic, swashbuckling tale. It is a time-dream play in which the main character, Peggy Willard, a high society girl, finds herself going back from persent day New Orleans to the time of the War of 1812.

Peggy sees her suitor, John Laffity, as too unromantic when compared with his ancestors, and so writer Herzig puts them both under the spell of a powerful voodoo potion that makes John dream he is his ancestor Jean Laffite, a buccaneer of renown. On his pirate ship, the buccaneer sails into the lagoon and captures Peggy, who is a famous ballerina. Of course they fall madly in love, but Peggy loses her man as the pirate turns honest and joins Andrew Jackson in defending New Orleans from the British.

Still under the spell, John becomes another of his ancestors, one Lucky Laffity, the gambler-owner of a New Orleans bistro. As it is 1905, a new sound called jazz is featured, which of course brings in Louis Armstrong and his All Stars. But Peggy's and John's love affair is again destroyed, this time by a character named Carrie Nation, the Kansas Hatchet Woman, and her followers.

The voodoo spell then wears off; John, however, is now stronger and more exciting, and Peggy finds he is the man of her dreams.

When Louis Armstrong came to Jones Beach, a tradition was born. Kenny explains: "It was silly to pay Louis to be in the play and only let him play five or ten minutes, so somebody came up with the bright idea of putting up a pavilion outside, next to the play area. Our band played the first half hour and that gave Louis and his band time to get offstage, and then they came out and played another half hour.

"Even after that show closed this dancing had been so well received that the tent was enlarged, the bandstand moved from one end to the center, and then we went on every night for an hour." This nightly dancing to the Royal Canadians' music continued as long as the Lombardo brothers produced the extravaganzas.

If it rained during the play, the production would be moved inside the tent.

The last summer that Guy, Carmen, and Lebert put on a show at Jones Beach was 1977. For years the work load had been piling up. Also, the brothers had merely broken even financially over the years and each year was a new worry. The weather presented the greatest problem. Alec Davidson says, "They worried about the weather every day. The *New York Times* would put out the weather report and call for rain, and that might be true for the city, but many times it was a moonlit night at Jones Beach. Many people wouldn't leave New York City if they thought it was going to rain. I remember listening to one of the broadcasts down there when the television announcer ended up saying, 'but not in Guy Lombardo's country.' "

After Guy's death in 1977, it was just too much for Lebert to run the Jones Beach productions alone. "You have no idea how many unions we have to deal with, stagehands, electricians, carpenters . . . Last year we did a show called *Finian's Rainbow*. Now it wasn't a very big cast, and we cut down our orchestra in the pit, but the break-even point was $1,500,000 in ticket sales. Now you have to get that back in nine and a half weeks. It's open air and just a worry, worry, worry."

In 1978, the Jones Beach productions were taken over by Westbury Music Fair.

Alec Davidson sums up the Lombardo business concerns over the years this way: "They've taken losses on many things, but always come out with no regrets because they've entertained, and that was their strong point, always concerned about whether they pleased people."

The Lombardo band has played every outstanding dancehall and pavilion in North America, including Carnegie Hall. But some of the Royal Canadians' best memories are of the White House in Washington where they played for presidents and kings and the Seventh Regiment Armory in New York City where they entertained queens and princesses.

One of Lebert's prize possessions, framed in silver and mounted behind glass, is a letter to Guy from Richard Nixon, thanking the Royal Canadians for playing at his inauguration. "We play all the inaugurals we're asked to. It's a great honor for us every time," Lebert says.

The band has been popular with politicians and presidents alike. Governor Dewey and Attorney General Brownell, among others, have danced to the "sweetest music this side of heaven." President Franklin Roosevelt heard the band while he was still governor of New York State, and it was he who first invited the Royal Canadians to play at an inaugural ball. "We were playing in 1931 at the Pavillon Royale in New York City where Ethel Merman got her start," Lebert explains. "We had closed the season and were going to New England. The owners of the Pavillon said to Guy, 'If you can possibly make it back, we're going to have a luncheon here for Roosevelt.' So we came back and the governor said, 'For doing this luncheon for me, if I'm elected president, you'll play the inaugural ball.'

THE WHITE HOUSE

WASHINGTON

March 12, 1973

Dear Guy:

The 1973 Inauguration was a huge success,
and certainly a great deal of credit for
that fact belongs to the superb quality of
the entertainment provided by an equally
outstanding group of performers.

I am deeply grateful to you and your band
for your willingness to take part in the
Inauguration. You did a great job at the
Inaugural Ball, and I know I speak for
every one in your audience in saying we
were delighted to have you with us.

With my best wishes to you and to the
members of your band,

Sincerely,

Richard Nixon

Mr. Guy Lombardo
7101 South Grove Street
Freeport, L.I., New York 11520

P.S. I thought you might like to have this
photograph of the Ball.

At the White House. Eleanor Roosevelt is in the center of the back row. Guy is seated second from the left. How many others can you recognize?

"At the Pavillon Royale, by the way, they had built a ramp for him. We didn't know he was paralyzed. They sort of kept it quiet."

Since the first Roosevelt inauguration, the band has played every inaugural to the present day, except for that of John F. Kennedy.

The Lombardo band was only one among many that played at each presidential inauguration. There are too many people invited to this gala event to be accommodated at a ball at the White House, so many balls go on in many places simultaneously. The White House, the Armory, the Pension Building, and the Smithsonian Institute, among other government edifices, are put into use for the festivities. So are the ballrooms of many hotels. In the course of the evening, the president, the first lady and their entourage visit each ball. Nowadays the Royal Canadians play at only one spot during the evening.

"In the old days it was different," Lebert says. "We'd play five or six places during one inaugural evening. We'd play the Shoreham Hotel for an hour, then go to another hotel, then an armory, all over the town. We had to follow the president."

For Kenny Gardner, the most exciting inaugural was that of Eisenhower. "That's because I'm a military man," he adds. However, it was not at the Eisenhower inaugural that Kenny chatted personally with the president but at a ball at the White House in honor of the state visit of a foreign king. Kenny relates, "We were playing in Burlington, Ontario in a dancehall on the water—it's gone now—but we were staying at a hotel in Hamilton. Well, our regular manager hadn't come along so I was doing the leg-work. In the early morning hours Guy, Carmen, and Lebert all got up and went somewhere. I came down to the lobby and as I went out to do some shopping the doorman said, 'Hi, Kenny.'

"Now as I came back, the doorman who had given me a very perfunctory hello before, my gosh, he snapped to attention and said, 'Mr. Gardner, there's an important call to you from Washington.' I walked in the door and the manager ran up. 'Mr. Gardner we have a call from the White House,' he said. 'Will you come right into my office?'

"The King of Siam, who's a saxophone player, was paying a state visit to Washington and he had requested that the Lombardo band play for a social function. 'Will you play for us?' the White House representative asked. Well of course the answer was Yes!"

Guy agreed to the change of itinerary and after several calls between the White House and the band's agent at MCA, the date and deal were struck. The president's luxurious plane, the Columbine, was sent to pick up the band and "Believe it or not," Kenny continues, "as we were approaching Dover, Delaware—it's a big air base—something happened to the plane. We were all looking out the window, and the air was full of planes. Whatever happened, they have a switch that someone at the airport pulls to tell everyone that the president's plane is in trouble. And so, as we looked out, planes started flying every direction and smoke and oil started pouring out of our engine. But we landed, and it's a funny thing, by the time we touched down and rolled to the gate, Washington had another Columbine ready and waiting to take us the rest of the way.

"They set us up in the East Room. We began to play and soon the king came in wearing all his medals. Vice-President Nixon was there, Senator Everett Dirksen was there, and so on. We played for an hour and pretty soon the king got up and walked all through the band as if on an inspection, but talking to all of us. He didn't play with us, but he did ask Carmen what kind of horn he had.

"After the party we went down to the lower level where there's a series of little oval rooms. We were sitting having coffee and cake and all of a sudden there was a knock at the door. One of the guys answered it and there was Eisenhower, all alone. He said, 'Hey, fellas, can I come in?' So you know, he came in and talked to us, each and every one of us, for the better part of an hour."

The Lombardos knew most of the influential politicians and businessmen of the time and they were on a first-name basis with many. Kenny knew John Eisenhower, Ike's son, very well. They had been in the same unit in the war. A few months after the band played for the king of Siam, John came to hear the Royal Canadians play and asked Kenny if he had mentioned their friendship to the president. Kenny said he had not.

Not only have presidents requested that the Lombardo band play at their inaugurals, but they have also come to view this as more than a tradition. Lyndon Johnson was the first president to come right onto the floor and dance. Later Nixon, Ford, and Carter followed suit.

"We were very honored," Lebert remembers, "when President Carter and his wife danced right in front of our band and asked Guy for 'Red Roses for a Blue Lady.' Mrs. Carter had on a blue dress. Vice-President Mondale also danced, not on the dance floor but up on the stage.

"We also played for Prime Minister Trudeau in Hamilton, Ontario. I think he's a terrific guy."

The night of one inaugural ball the fog closed tightly over Washington, and the chartered plane that was to take all the bands that had played at the various locations back to New York City could not take off. After spending the night in Washington, the bands took off the next morning. On board were the Lombardo band, the Count Basie band, the Lawrence Welk band, and the Leo Reitman band. Shortly after takeoff the fog once more filled the sky, and the pilot circled and circled above New York City for many hours before he could land. Getting out of the plane, the Lombardo band were thankful that they had landed at all as the visibility was zero. Guy turned to his band and quipped somewhat nervously, "My God, if we had crashed and it had wiped us all out, the only band left would be Sammy Kaye!"

Another tremendous thrill for the Royal Canadians were the Commonwealth balls held in the Seventh Regiment Armory in New York City. For the Canadian Lombardo brothers, this was a dream come true. The kindly royal faces, above chests adorned with blaz-

At an inaugural ball.

ing purple sashes, that had shone down upon them in their classrooms back at St. Peter's Separate School in London, Ontario, were now shining straight at them in person. It was enough to rattle even the normally calm and casual Guy Lombardo.

The first Commonwealth ball was in honor of the present Queen Mother, Elizabeth, consort to the late King George VI. Kenny and Elaine remember the evening vividly. The band was set up on a huge bandstand near the entrance to the hall. Across the dance floor was the royal dais. Elaine remembers the dignity of the Queen Mother, resplendent in sashes and jewels. "You get that feeling of royalty and exactly who they are," says Lebert. Kenny speaks for all the Royal Canadians as he describes the evening.

"The boys in the band had a saying, 'You name it, we've done it, seen it, heard it, or been there.' They were pretty blasé guys, and the old-timers could play a part. Well, it came time for the Queen Mother's entrance and someone started blowing bugles, and in she came. Now she came around and stood in front of the bandstand, looked up and, so help me, each and every guy in the band damn near wilted. She had that look. She looked at everybody and Buddy Brennan and everyone else said, 'She looked right at me! I know she looked right at me!' Guy just wilted, and Carmen started adjusting his tie. He always did that when he was nervous. Then the Queen Mother nodded very graciously and walked all the way around the room to the royal stand. She had an equerry with her dressed in a Scottish outfit, not a kilt, but pants. She signaled to him, and he walked up to her, and she whispered something. Then he did what we call the 'British stomp.' He turned around and walked right across the doggone ballroom floor. We knew he was coming to us, and sure enough he walked right up to Guy and said, 'Her Majesty requests "Hernando's Hideaway." ' I had to get up and walk down the stage, and I'm telling you, I'm a pretty cool character, but even I was shaking.''

A year later the Lombardo band played another Commonwealth ball in the Seventh Regiment Armory in New York. This time, however, the guests of honor were Queen Elizabeth II and Prince Philip. The play *My Fair Lady* was the rage at this time all over North America and special *My Fair Lady* tuxedos were designed for the occasion. As a matter of record, Guy often had tuxedos or jackets made up to suit special occasions. To the band members, who had all just been to see the movie *Roman Holiday* in which Audrey Hepburn played a queen, this was an evening of quiet dignity and grace. The band was very impressed by the Duke of Edinburgh. Prince Philip told the band members that he had several of their records and regularly played them at Buckingham Palace. A couple of the Royal Canadians had known the Earl of Mountbatten, and they compared the prince to his uncle.

The Royal Canadians were to have played one other time for Queen Elizabeth. The occasion was to mark the opening of the St. Lawrence Seaway. Plans called for the band to fly from New York to Canada, meeting the queen who would be sailing up the St. Lawrence River in her royal yacht. Fog, the curse of all who travel as often as the Royal Canadians, prevented the plane from landing, and the boat from sailing. The Royal Canadians were sorely disappointed that they did not get to play for Her Majesty on this occasion.

Guy Lombardo's Royal Canadians continue to play dancehalls and state occasions. When asked if the band will play the next inaugural ball, Lebert looks up quickly and emphatically replies, "I hope so!"

11
Brothers and Bandsmen

✩ ✩ ✩ ✩ ✩ ✩ ✩ ✩ ✩ ✩ ✩ ✩

"When you are talking about the band," Alec Davidson recalls, "you have to admit, Carmen was the boss. He had to hear the sound that he wanted and he had to put phrasing together. Guy wouldn't agree at the time maybe, but I have seen Carmen stamp his foot. After all, he knew more about music than Guy."

Carmen was a flutist in their London days, a very fine flutist. However, he was very interested in the early American dance bands and through his interest heard of the saxophone. In the twenties it was still seen in the United States as a weird contraption, a funny sort of reed instrument. Carmen wanted to try everything, and it is reputed that he was one of the first people to import a saxophone into Canada.

There was no one to teach him the instrument so he used the same mouthings he had used on the flute. Carmen talked with a vibrato sound and his voice quivered a little. This came through in his saxophone playing.

The Lombardo fans loved to hear Carmen sing. It was just this vibrato that so intrigued them. *The Diners' Club Magazine* described his voice as "resembling a plate of Jello confronted by a strong wind." His voice was as much a Royal Canadians' trademark as the slow tempo or the quiet rhythm section.

Carmen's voice appealed especially to young fans. One young man, back in the thirties, strode purposefully up to the bandstand at the Roosevelt Grill and complained angrily that his girlfriend

The famous saxophone trio: Fred (Derf) Higman, Carmen Lombardo, and Cliff Grass.

wanted to come night after night to the grill because "she says Carmen's voice does things to her."

Whenever Guy, pushed by Decca Records, asked guest singers like the Andrews Sisters or Evelyn Knight to be on their recordings, the fans would be affronted. They wanted the pure Lombardo sound, and that meant either Carmen or Kenny Gardner singing.

Carmen didn't like to sing. He much preferred just to play his instruments. Moreover, other singers and comedians made fun of his voice. The talented blind singer and mimic, Alec Templeton, used to mimic Carmen's vibrato voice. They found the "quivering gibraltor" voice especially funny.

In spite of Carmen's reticence he became a well-loved part of the Lombardo sound. The early trio, consisting of the three sax players,

Carmen, Larry Owen, and Derf Higman, had voices that blended together like honey. Later on, Kenny Gardner sang as part of the trio when Larry left to join Jan Garber's band in California. After Carmen died and Derf Higman retired, Cliff Grass and Joe Cipriano took over with Kenny as the Lombardo trio. Although their sound was obviously not the same as their original counterparts, they were *extremely* popular. "I get a thrill even yet hearing that old trio on record," Alec Davidson says. "It reminds me of the days when I'd come home from skating, and they'd be on the radio for Esso or someone else like that, and I'd think 'What a nice sound that is!' "

Even after Kenny Gardner became the singer with Guy Lombardo's Royal Canadians, Carmen would still have to put down his sax and come to the microphone to sing songs such as "Boo Hoo" and "The Three Little Fishes (Itty Bitty Poo)."

In the early days, the arrangements were made as a family affair,

Courtesy of Alec Davidson

Victor, Carmen, Lebert, and Guy photographed by their friend, Alec Davidson, during the 1950s.

each member having his say about his instrument's part. The Royal Canadians did not have arrangers on a regular basis until the 1930s.

Carmen was a gentle, intellectual man. When the band first moved to New York City, Carmen began talking to songwriters and reporters. He wanted to become a more fluent and articulate speaker. The brothers, if they wanted to find Carmen, would look for him in a library, either at the Roosevelt Hotel or the Metropolitan New York Library. He'd look up unfamiliar words that he had heard, knowing that he not only needed to converse properly, he needed a great range of words for his songs.

Carmen's favorite game was backgammon and he once wrote a book on the subject. He was interested in business and held a seat on the New York Stock Exchange in the 1930s. Anything that involved detailing intrigued Carmen. He would talk about any subject in great detail, standing nose-to-nose to the person with whom he was conversing, taking every bit of attention the person had to offer.

Unlike Guy, who loved the speed and challenge of speedboat racing, Carmen loved the calm and quiet of sailing.

Carmen and his wife, Florence, "a woman you could warm up to," according to sister-in-law Elaine, were childless.

During the fifties, when Carmen wrote a song titled "Our Little Ranch House," they built themselves a ranch-style home in Woodmere, Long Island. Decorated by brother Joe, it was beautifully furnished but in spite of all their success, Carmen and Florence were not ostentatious. While he could have afforded a huge home and big car, Carmen had a home suited for the two of them and he drove a Limited Ford. Later he bought a chocolate-colored Mercedes.

In 1969 gentle, uncomplaining Carmen, who had never been seriously ill, began to get irritable and tired. An examination by the famed Dr. Michael E. Debakey of Houston's Methodist Hospital revealed the reason why. Carmen had a stomach cancer.

For the next year and a half Carmen flew back to Houston for treatments, but was able to travel most of the time with the band. John Miller, a freelance writer traveling with the band on assignment in 1970, wrote of Carmen's reaction to a dance he had driven up from Methodist Hospital to see. From a tape cassette of the dance Miller writes, "Carmen called Guy from Houston to complain that a certain section of the band was a fraction late on the pick-up on the sixteenth note of 'Harbor Lights.' Guy taped the phone conversation and the next morning played it to members of the band. The phone call included Carmen's singing of the number up to the sixteenth note, so as to pinpoint the error."

The last New Year that Carmen was to ring in was 1971. "I saw him once more during his illness," Alec Davidson says. "The band was playing in Toronto at the Royal York Hotel for a week and he flew up with Florence. He walked in thin and slow and sat at the table in the dark opposite the bandstand. It was a sad thing because he sat there looking very frail. He wanted to hear them once more. That was it; he wanted to hear them again. Guy introduced him and the spotlight shone on him. He stood up with that nice smile of his and then he left. I spoke to him the next day, but you could see that he was at the end." In April, 1971 Carmen died. Florence would follow him a few years later in 1973, dying in Florida at their North Shore condominium.

When Carmen died, the dance bands lost a valuable songwriter. He had collaborated with composers Gus Kahn and Joe Young in writing such hits as "Powder Your Face with Sunshine," "Sweethearts on Parade," and "Little Coquette." His major songwriting partner since 1936 was John Jacob Loeb, who died in 1970. Loeb had composed such songs as "Masquerade," "Reflections," and "The Maharajah of Magador." With Loeb, Carmen produced the best-selling tunes "Boo Hoo," "A Sailboat in the Moonlight," and "Ma, I Miss Your Apple Pie." Their most famous tune perhaps is "Seems Like Old Times," which, of course, was Arthur Godfrey's theme song. The recent movie, *Annie Hall*, starring Woody Allen and Diane Keaton, featured "Seems Like Old Times" as its theme. The Lombardo-Loeb songs are now proving popular with the grandchildren of the songwriters' original audience.

Dewey Bergman reflects on the limitations forced on a songwriter of Carmen's generation. "It used to be you'd have to write a thirty-two bar song. If you wrote a sixty-four bar song they would throw you out of a publishing house. Today they don't count the bars, they just keep going . . ."

Most of all Bergman remembers the closeness between Carmen and Guy. "When Carmen passed away Guy didn't face the band for at least six or eight months. He beat the band off with his back to them. Carmen used to beat the band off. Guy would give the downbeat, but Carmen beat the band off with his foot. You could set a stopwatch. They had three tempos, slow, medium, and fast. You would know the slow tempo would last fifty-five seconds."

Radio Guide magazine had written of Carmen in 1933. "He . . . does things with a saxophone that would turn Sebastian Sax (or was Johannes Sax?) a bright green with bitter envy. He not only plays saxophone but he sings, as four quarters of the radio globe will tell you. He sings well."

The article continues, "Carmen has just rushed in with the information that it was neither Sebastian nor Johannes Sax who invented the saxophone, it was Antoine Joseph Sax. It doesn't matter. It could have been Siegfried Sax and Carmen would have been just as elegant at the work of making music come out of the instrument."

Carmen's death was the first among the Lombardo children. They had lived to see Mama and Papa grow old and, in a memorable evening in 1951, had toasted Mama's and Papa's fiftieth wedding anniversary. Two years later, Papa died of a heart attack. Mama followed him the year after.

Lebert, in his seventies, is full of vigor and laughter. Of the brothers, he is the most spontaneous, the first to laugh at a joke. Lebert is energetic and in a hurry, but relaxed.

He is a fine, fine musician. He plays the trumpet as if born to it, as if his instrument were part of him. He is so good in fact that during the Detroit days, Jean Goldkette, who desperately wanted Lebert in his band, offered Guy two trumpeters, a sax player, and $200 a week in exchange for Lebert and his horn.

Lebert is the only one of the three brothers to have children. In fact he had seven, four from his first marriage to Helen Healey, an oil heiress from Bradford, Pennsylvania. One of the four is Bill Lombardo, the current leader of the Royal Canadians. This marriage, unfortunately, ended in divorce. In 1953 Lebert married Peggy Landers, according to Kenny Gardner "a little Texas girl,

Courtesy of Lebert Lombardo

Mama's and Papa's fiftieth wedding anniversary in 1951.

Courtesy of Garth Scheuer

Lebert Lombardo in 1978.

just lovely. They used to call her the Startled Fawn." Lebert called Peggy every night he was on the road, he was so fond of her. She died in 1973. Out of this marriage came three more children who live with Lebert in Amityville, Long Island. They are Lizanne, born in 1955, Gina, born in 1960, and Carmen, born in 1962.

Lebert is a shy man but still gregarious. Guy once said, "We're a clannish family. We don't entertain. After all, that's what I do for a living." When friends came to Jones Beach they always ended up at Lebert's home. He loves to be with people, to be affectionate, and to receive affection.

"Lebert was a camera buff, a moving picture buff," Bern Davies remembers. "He had a moving picture machine and we lived in Kew Gardens at the time in New York, before any of the parkways were in, in 1928 or 1929. We were recording one day down at the old Victor recording studio at Union Square and he says, 'Hey, take a look at this!' Over in the corner was a talking picture machine. Now, the talkies didn't come in until later and this was a 'sound on film.' Before that, any sound was on wax. They'd cut a wax disk and synchronize it with the pictures. 'That doesn't look too tough,' Lebe said. 'Do you think we can make one?' I said we could sure try

Courtesy of Lebert Lombardo

Lebert with all his children in 1962.

because I was rather mechanical and so we borrowed—we couldn't buy one—a photoelectric cell like the one in this machine. We never did get an optical cell. We had to improvise and make that! He bought a Halls projector for a couple of hundred dollars and I built a talking picture machine onto the side of it. The fellows at Eveready who loaned us the photo cell said that we had the first home talking machine in the world.

"Lebe was always doing things like that with moving pictures. The bloody thing caught on fire once in an apartment in Forest Hills, New York, and darn near burned the apartment down. He wasn't supposed to have this thirty-five millimeter film in the apartment and of course we ran and buried the film so the fire marshal couldn't find it. I guess he knew what caused it, but he couldn't find the film!

"We were playing in vaudeville in those days and Lebe'd go up to the projection booth, and they'd give him the weekly *Pathé News*. He had thousands of feet of celluloid film in that apartment!"

Today Lebert is the only one of the nine original Royal Canadians. He says that he will stick with the band until his son Bill is established as bandleader. Then Lebert would like to retire and spend more time at home with his younger children.

The youngest brother, Victor, who joined the band in 1930, is a casual, informal man. He remained with the band for over twenty-five years with two or three intervals when he led his own band. Today, Victor lives with his second wife, Cathy, in Florida where he has his own group. His first wife, Ginny, died in 1973 and he has two grown sons. "I'll tell you about Victor," Kenny says. "First off, as a musician he was one of the finest, the steadiest, the most reliable, the most consistent and dependable musicians that I have ever heard in my life. Victor was always there and *always*, whenever Carmen couldn't make it for whatever reason, Victor could step in and it took an expert to tell the difference between the two. That was Victor at his best.

"You have to understand," he continues, "it's a little bit of psychology. If you have a family with lots of kids in it, the youngest kid is trying to emulate, outachieve, or at least attain the same rate of achievement, as his elder brothers and sisters. The youngest one is always striving to catch up. That's why they say the youngest one seems to walk earlier, talk sooner, and all that. Now that was the case with Victor. Victor came in after his brothers had had their big nationwide success. All *they* were interested in from then on was in maintaining their place in the sun as it were. Victor had yet to make *his* place in the sun. All his life Victor always felt that he could make a contribution to the band, that he could have his own band, that he could do this or that he could do that, and his elder brothers only wanted to keep and maintain what they had! So as it went along, it began to get to Victor. He started his own band at the wrong time. He came back again when Carmen became ill and played just perfectly. There were things that had to be done and the elder brothers said, 'No we can't do them. We're going to keep it exactly as it is,' and pretty soon Victor just said, 'There's nothing here; I've got to go.' He did very well on his own at the time, but the dance-band business as the great glittering tiara we once knew is gone. So he had his own troubles.

"When Guy died, we needed Victor. We really needed his sense of perfection, his sense of constancy. We needed whatever he had. We really welcomed him back. But again here came that old thing.

He had no respect for what the band was, what it had attained or achieved and he wanted to change it. So Lebert just put his foot down and said, 'No, I'm not going to change it! However far or however short a time I've got to go, we're going exactly the way we always did, the way Guy would have wanted!' But Victor couldn't see that, and it just kept building, and finally again he just said, 'Aw, I can't take this,' and he left. I think Victor had a very great contribution to make, but he just couldn't overcome all of his desires, wishes, and ambitions and he just couldn't blend them into this set, this concrete, this monolithic thing that was the Lombardo band.

"He is a fine musician. I could go through dozens of our orchestrations and records and point out, that's Victor, that's Victor, that's Victor, and you can see how much an essential part he was."

Over the years, the original Royal Canadians have left the band. Muff Henry, guitar player, who wrote the popular song "Little Girl" died in 1959. Freddie Kreitzer left the band in 1968. He had had four operations on his hands and simply felt the touring was too much for him. He now lives in Florida. He has no piano in his house and rarely touches the organ his wife gave him. George Gowans first retired in 1971. Later, Guy called him and asked him to come back for a few weeks. George stayed for two years and retired permanently to Florida in 1976. Derf Higman retired in 1967 to open a furniture store named the Wagon Wheel on Long Island.

Hugo D'Ippolito, whose father had given Carmen saxophone lessons in London, was the original second piano of the twin pianos, but he left the band after an altercation with Guy. Alec Davidson tells the story: "They had made a deal, almost back in 1929 that they would put a rose in their lapels every night and Hugo refused to wear one. This was before the red uniform. One thing led to another with Hugo; he wasn't going to do that kind of stuff. He was rebellious. He was perhaps a better musician than most of them in the band. He'd studied more music. I think he thought he knew more. But he didn't make the sound; he was part of it."

Hugo left the band in the thirties. Francis Vino, who played the harpsicord as well, then took over the second piano. Buddy Brennan, a graduate of the Juilliard School of Music, came to the band and stayed for more than seven years. Many observers have said the twin pianos had more sparkle under Freddie and Buddy than with any other combination. Many other pianists played opposite Freddie. It was the large amount of roadwork that made many musicians leave the band.

A singer who was with the band in the fifties came out of the

The famous Lombardo twin pianos, Freddie Kreitzer, left, and Hugo D'Ippolito.

Fred Waring orchestra. Guy first noticed Bill Flannagan when he was playing with a U.S. Navy band at the Canadian National Exhibition in Toronto. Flannagan played the trombone and euphonium as well as being a singer. When he left the navy he joined Fred Waring's Pennsylvanians where Guy sought him out and recruited him. While he was with the band, he played all his instruments, including the guitar, and sang. Today he leads his own group in Florida.

Tony Cointreau, grandson of the founder of the Cointreau liqueur company, sang with the band at Tierra Verde. He sang out of a sheer love of entertaining.

Dudley Fozdick was an interesting musician who invented an instrument he called the fozophone, a mellophone he had twisted and rolled to make the sound he wanted. Fozdick played with the band for about four years during the mid-thirties. He never played an arrangement the same way twice. At first Guy didn't like this variation, but couldn't complain because Fozdick, although playing in his own way, always made the music fit the Lombardo sound and style. He was a very good musician. Later Fozdick apparently joined an eastern-style religious cult in Arizona.

Fozdick didn't like the sun. "I remember Derf saying that if the sun was shining, when they got off the bus, he'd bring his jacket and put it over the top of his head. He'd stay in the shade," Alec Davidson relates.

Bern Davies retired from the band in 1951. "I had a wife and a young daughter at this time and I was never home for Christmas, New Year's, or our anniversary. I was never home. The night I quit the band was going out on ninety-one straight one-nighters. When I walked off the stand, I put the horn in the case and I haven't seen it from that day to this. It's up in the attic." Today Davies sells real estate in Florida.

Of course, because of the frequent changeovers in band personnel, it is impossible to name all the members or give their stories here. Even Guy realized that. He once said, "We have a change about every year. When you look at twelve pictures, you've got the whole band." He did not try to keep band photos up to date. Realistically he said, "They'll remember the old ones better than the new ones."

Though none of the original members, save Lebert, are in the band today, the orchestra has the same soft tempo, quivering sax, and crystal-clear trumpet sound. Bill Lombardo, the new bandleader, is sticking to a sound and format that he knows works well.

Courtesy of the Long Island State Park and Recreation Commission

The silvery trumpets of the Royal Canadians play at Jones Beach Marine Theatre in 1960. The show was *Hit the Deck*.

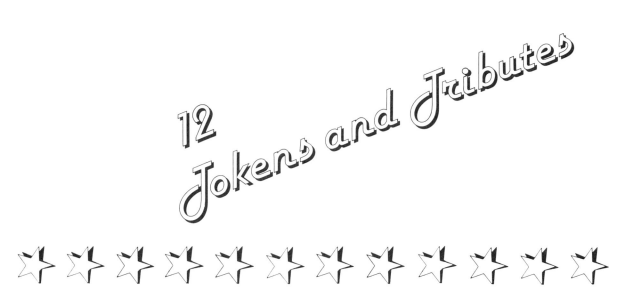

12 Tokens and Tributes

Guy Lombardo's Royal Canadians have been honored by happy dancers every night they have played over the past sixty years. Guy once said, "Nobody likes my music but my fans." He didn't care who said what about him, including the music critics, as long as his fans kept loving him.

In almost every town, fans would ask to see Guy and his brothers, bringing such gifts as handmade wooden replicas of his speedboat, miniature violins, saxophones, or trumpets. The brothers, always on tour and always on the run, were genuinely thrilled to receive these tokens of esteem.

As well, the Lombardo band has been given the keys to hundreds of cities and towns in North America. Many of these souvenirs were on display at Guy Lombardo's East Point House Restaurant in Freeport, Long Island, and lost when the restaurant burned down.

"It was a funny thing," recalls Kenny Gardner. "Guy was very lax about these objects because I guess he kind of thought the band would never end, it would go on forever. About putting trophies away he always said, 'I'll get to it some day,' but he never did."

Lebert still has many of these gifts at his home in Amityville. His daughter Lizanne, the family archivist, is currently sorting and arranging the Royal Canadian mementos.

Most of the honors the band received were given to Guy on behalf of his Royal Canadians. Guy, of course, was the front man, but without brothers Carmen and Lebert, original musicians such

Courtesy of Saul Richman

Guy and Lebert shortly before Guy's death.

as Freddie and George, and distinctive personalities such as Kenny Gardner, the band never would have attained its brilliantly successful sound.

Kenny himself won the annual *Downbeat* magazine award in 1959 for the best male band singer in a poll conducted for the National Ballroom Operators' Association. He had always considered being one of Guy Lombardo's Royal Canadians an honor in itself. He remembers how frightened he first was of joining this particular band. "I know when I first came into the band I had already been in the business for a long, long time under very harsh circumstances and I knew all about it. When I joined I knew the band's value, its status, its stature, and I was scared I'd do something that would damage that."

Most of the quiet charity work of the band has not been made public. Guy did hundreds of free radio spots, lending his name on behalf of children's societies, hospital building funds, and war veteran appeals. During the war itself the band performed often, soliciting civilians to buy war bonds and other war support articles. On these occasions, every girl who came to hear them with an enlisted man was admitted free and Guy would play patriotic songs all night.

In 1960, the Lombardo brothers produced the play *Hit the Deck* at the Jones Beach Marine Theatre and they asked Commander S. Jessie Robinson of the Freeport Naval Reserve Training Center to be the play's technical advisor and coordinator of naval relations. On opening night, 400 men from the center took part in the play. That same summer, Vice-Admiral Charles Wellborn Jr. presented Guy with a certificate of appreciation from the Third District Naval Administration for his help in the Navy recruiting program.

As mentioned earlier, Guy mixed with legendary show business greats, and in 1977 he took his place among them. His foot and hand prints were recorded in the Stars' Hall of Fame at Orlando, Florida. After receiving the honor, Lombardo joked, "The last time I put my feet in cement I was eight years old in London, Ontario and I think I got spanked for it." The Stars' Hall of Fame, incidentally, also includes life-size wax figures of 180 movie, television, and recording stars.

In 1959, Labatt's Ltd., the brewery company, whose retail store stands on the site of the boys' childhood Horton Street home, unveiled a plaque in honor of the Lombardo boys. The four brothers, Guy, Carmen, Lebert, and Victor, were all present at the unveiling and each pulled a golden cord that opened the doors of the plaque. Immediately on the pulling of the cord, the theme song "Auld Lang Syne" emanated from the plaque. "This is the most memorable moment of my life," Guy said that day. He was truly moved as he listened to Labatt's president, S. H. Moore say the following words: "Despite all the success you have enjoyed, the public acclaim you have received, the international honors which have been accorded you, the early days and the old friends in London have not been forgotten. We at Labatt's hope this plaque will be a permanent monument to those early days when the climb was still ahead of you and to those friends who helped and encouraged you." The ceremony was held in the parking lot at the rear of the store where so many years ago the four brothers had escaped from under Papa's watchful eye to play ball.

Although the Royal Canadians have never left North America, they have royal admirers and fans all over the world. Even

Victor, Lebert, Guy and Carmen unveil a plaque marking the site of the Lombardos' boyhood home in London, Ontario.

Courtesy of Labbatt's Ltd.

Courtesy of Sam McLeod of the London Free Press

Bandleader Guy Lombardo, a native of London, was honored at the University of Western Ontario's spring convocation when he received an honorary doctor of music degree. He is hooded by Clifford von Kuster, right, dean of the UWO faculty of music. At left is university chancellor, Dr. Albert Trueman.

Emperor Haile Selassie of Ethiopia, who walked with Guy on the Long Island boardwalk, presented Guy with a personal medal.

On May 25, 1971, Guy Lombardo received what he called the greatest honor of his life. The boy from London, Ontario, who had only finished grade school, the boy whose father had always urged his sons to strive for the top, was awarded an honorary doctorate of music from the University of Western Ontario in London. Accompanied by a friend, actress Julia Mead, and his brother, Joe, he flew in from a tour to receive the award. Guy gave a spontaneous speech to more than 500 fellow graduates in Western's Alumni Hall and told them of his father who urged his sons "to learn something of music." He told the students of his father's advice: "Always do more work than you are paid for," and advised them to do the same.

The university's president, Dr. D. Carleton Williams, in his citation, said: "The delightful irony of this day lies in the fact that in the midst of all its hastening change, it has taken this university over forty years to catch up with a man who in his public life has not changed at all . . . Our distinguished graduand achieved early in life what many artists spend their lives searching for, a unique, distinctive, and recognizable style.

". . . There are present with us today a host of his old friends, several of whom, once upon a time, hired the band for the staggering sum of twenty-five dollars a night. Again there are those who vividly recall the famous story of the only time the band failed to appear as promised. When the frantic convenor personally ran to the Lombardo home, she was informed firmly by their mother that the boys would be late because they had neglected to take out the ashes . . . The Royal Canadians never forgot the city of their birth, as demonstrated by their return to London at their own expense to play a series of benefit concerts for the victims of the disastrous flood of 1937.

". . . Were I to design a coat of arms for the Lombardo band its field would clearly be the Canadian flag surmounted by royal crowns, the whole supported by a pair of crossed saxophones. The motto, of course, would be inevitable: *Symphoniam dei audiunt soli suaviorem*; which translates, 'Only the gods hear sweeter music.' This is as close to 'The sweetest music this side of heaven' as Latin can come, but then, the ancient Romans never heard the Royal Canadians."

Guy was always a humble man. Jean Lombardo, wife of Hubert Lombardo, Guy's first cousin who still lives in London, remembers the day he received this honor. "We went out to Howard Johnson's after he received his doctorate. We were sitting having a drink and

Photo by Beverly Fink Cline

Hubert and Jean Lombardo of London, Ontario, who gave much help in preparing this book.

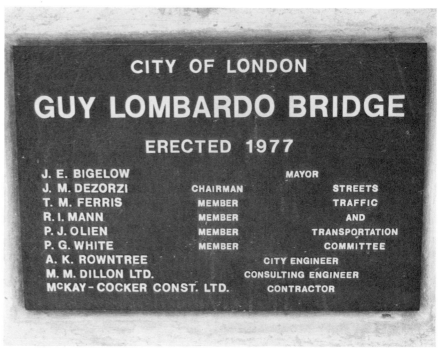

Courtesy of Leigh Cline

I told him what a wonderful speech he'd made, and he said, 'Do you think it was all right Jean?' and I thought, 'Here's the great Guy asking Jean Lombardo!' The speech was excellent. He just said the right thing."

After Guy's death, London City Council decided to name a bridge after him. On November 16, 1978 Hubert Lombardo officially opened the Guy Lombardo bridge.

In June, 1978, the officials of Freeport, Long Island decided to change the name of South Grove Street, where Guy had lived for so many years, to Guy Lombardo Avenue. Furthermore, they redesignated Freeport Long Creek Marina as Guy Lombardo Marina.

Guy's widow, Lilliebell, was prevented from attending the name changing ceremonies because of a broken shoulder. However, the late Saul Richman Publicity Director of the Royal Canadians, did attend and read a speech on Mrs. Lombardo's behalf. Mrs. Lombardo said how proud she was of the honors bestowed on Guy and added, "I have a feeling that Guy is with you in spirit today. And the humming of the boats along the Marina and the sound of a child laughing on the street that both now carry his name will always give me continued pleasure and consolation and an ever-present nearness to him." Clearly, Mrs. Lombardo was moved.

The Royal Canadians still receive many, many honors today.

New Year's Eve 1978 was the fiftieth year that the band had rung in the New Year over the air. Led by Bill Lombardo, the band was feted to honor this happy and memory-laden anniversary.

On the afternoon of December 14, 1978, Fiftieth St. and Park Ave., New York, were closed to traffic and the Royal Canadians performed in the open air, close to the Waldorf-Astoria. The street was festooned with banners proclaiming the band's fiftieth anniversary.

In addition, Kenny Gardner, who had retired the previous spring, came back to appear on the New Year's Eve Program commemorating his thirty-eight years with the band.

Guy Lombardo's Royal Canadians have grown over fifty years from a two-brother duo to a world-renowned popular dance band. Papa had set his boys in the right direction!

Guy Lombardo, June 19, 1902—November 5, 1977.

Guy had lived seventy-five years, sixty-two of which he had spent as a bandleader.

His death came as a shock to North Americans. The man was an institution, and institutions certainly don't die.

Guy Lombardo was a hard-driving man. He lived his days fully. In fact, he was so busy, so involved, that reporters assigned to do articles on him often complained that they couldn't keep up with him! Alan Edmonds, in his article on Guy of October 27, 1962, in the Toronto *Star Weekly* wrote, "In that weekend he flew in from a business trip to St. Louis; spent six painstaking hours at a recording session; twice appeared on television; twice worked with the cast of Paradise Isle late into the night, and squeezed in time to attend a dinner party, watch a televised baseball game and talk about the orchestra."

Guy had been a hard taskmaster in the early days of the band. He wanted to succeed, he knew his band members wanted to succeed, and with his characteristic punch he drove them. However, it must be pointed out in all honesty that he never asked his band members to work harder or longer than he himself was willing to do, and the band called him the Old Man affectionately.

He was also temperamental and would holler back and forth with both his brothers and the original band members from Lon-

Guy talks to the Jones Beach audience on the opening night of *Song of Norway* in 1958.

don and Cleveland. Bern Davies says, "I used to get fired every month over a period of twenty years. I remember one occasion during the war years. The windows were tightly curtained to black out the lights and we had to finish at midnight. We used to have a great many of the wartime high brass in the audience. One night at twelve the Old Man gave us the motion to stand up and play the national anthem. I stood up with my horn and put one foot on my chair. I sat on the very right-hand side where the steps go down to the dance floor. There's a brass railing there and right in the middle of this bloody thing when we came into the trio, the center section of 'The Star-Spangled Banner,' my foot slipped off the chair and I fell down and the horn went bouncing down this darn railing and jumped onto the floor. Right in this soft, very patriotic thing—the generals were saluting and everything—and the Old Man looked over at me and said, 'You're fired,' and that broke up the whole band. Of course, they couldn't play. I just came the next night. I think it's fun to talk about these old things."

It's been said that all bandleaders are prima donnas. Perhaps this is true, but as one musician pointed out, "The bandleaders have to put up with musicians talking behind their backs, grumbling and so on."

Guy always asserted that one of the reasons the Lombardo sound was so identifiable and so popular was that the musicians were able to work together so well. They did not lose their first men or originals for so many years. "Other bands lose their first men, have to change around, lose their identifying style, but we've stayed together," Guy once said.

Guy helped out the band members if they needed assistance. He saw them through financial crises, alcoholism, family squabbles, and hurt musical egos. He was a kind man and saw his band as an extended family.

At home with Lilliebell, his wife of fifty-one years, Guy Lombardo lived in a manorial yet extremely comfortable and informal home designed by his brother, Joe. Located in the actors' colony at Freeport, Long Island, the home, screened by high hedges, sits on a lot the size of one square block.

Guy was a homebody when he had the time. He could "do a crossword puzzle with his eyes closed," remembered the late Saul Richman, the band's publicity director for many years.

Another hobby was putting pins in a huge map to mark every place in the world from which a fan letter had been received. As early as 1933, the Lombardo band broadcasts had been transmitted on shortwave from the States, and this opened up a whole world of fans.

Courtesy of Saul Richman

Guy relaxes behind the scenes.

Lilliebell, a beautifully delicate woman, is reserved and takes good care of her own privacy. She has been active in charity work though she is careful where she lends her famous name. As she returned late from a club meeting one night in 1947, Kirk, the Lombardo's pet great dane, thinking she was an intruder, sprang at her and bit her face. Although she required plastic surgery to save her from permanent disfigurement, Mrs. Lombardo refused to punish the dog as he was only doing his duty in protecting the Lombardo home.

Mrs. Lombardo was always very influential in determining the band's sound and choice of music. The late Saul Richman said that Guy used to call her every night while he was on the road, ask her opinion of their radio shows, and that he took her advice and opinions very seriously. "If I don't like new numbers or arrangements, Guy usually scraps them," she once said. "I've usually been right, but when I did make a mistake, it was a lulu: I thought the public wouldn't like 'Little White Lies.'"

Guy spent all the time he could at home with Lilliebell. He seldom attended "jam sessions," preferring to spend his few nights off at home.

Five feet six inches tall, Guy was not a good-looking man in the conventional sense, yet in the 1930s he was known as the Lothario of Music. As he got older, rigorous dieting and his full days kept

On the set of *Mardi Gras* in 1965.

him in shape. One critic of the Lombardo sound—and the brothers had many—once said that Guy always looked young because of the sleep he got while leading his band. This was hardly the case.

Over the fifty years he led the Royal Canadians, critics gave Guy various nicknames: the King of Corn, Gabriel's Maestro, and Gooey Lumbago. Guy never cared what his critics said. First, with such a large number of loyal fans he had cause to feel secure. More important, Guy had no illusions about his band's music. "I know my band isn't the cleverest or the most shocking. When someone says, 'You've got a great band,' I know he isn't telling the truth. But when he says, 'That was a beautiful song,' I'm thrilled for I know I've been playing music that lingers in the hearts of my listeners."

He always maintained that he saw no reason to change his style and compared his band to the New York Yankees under Joe McCarthy. Why should he change his lineup when he's winning? "Swing is for adolescents," he maintained. "Romantic music is for all ages, all times."

In September, 1977, Guy entered Houston's Methodist Hospital. All that summer Guy had seemed fine, but his brother-in-law, Kenny Gardner, remembers, "I have a nickname around here, and it comes from being able to see things objectively. All last summer I would come home here at night after the Jones Beach job and I would tell Elaine, 'There's something radically wrong with Guy.' Friends would say, 'Well, we saw him last night. He sounds good,' and I'd say 'Nope,' and I'd come home and Elaine would call me Calamity Kenny. I said, 'I don't know what it is, I'm no doctor, but I know there is something wrong.' "

"I think Guy was worried," Elaine continues. "He probably knew and he didn't want to go down to Houston."

The Royal Canadians went back on a road tour of Canada without Guy. A report, unofficial and unconfirmed by Lombardo representatives, began to circulate that Freddy Martin was coming to lead the band instead of Guy. Like all rumors this one grew and grew until, as Elaine says, "The report was that instead of Guy Lombardo, Freddy Martin was coming, and the people thought that meant Freddy Martin's band. One lady who came to the show said her husband didn't come with her. He had said, 'I'm not going. I don't want to hear the Freddy Martin band.' She said that if it wasn't the Guy Lombardo band she would ask for her money back. She told us when she came right backstage. When she saw Kenny and all the boys she realized that Guy wasn't there, but it was the Lombardo band."

As soon as the Royal Canadians returned to the United States, a booker came to their motel to meet with them. He said, "Kenny, I've set up a couple of radio interviews so I want you to come to the station and make it clear that everybody in the band, the twin pianos, Lebert, all the band, will be there. It is the Lombardo band."

Kenny did the interviews, calling ahead to places such as San Francisco and San Jose.

In September Guy was back at Houston again, and Dr. Michael E. Debakey, the man who has also tended Carmen, performed open-heart surgery. Guy was a very sick man, but he was determined to get well quickly and return to the band. "I'll keep on playing until they put me underground," Guy once said. When he was released from the hospital and came home, "everybody in the band perked up," Kenny remembers. "We thought, gee, the Old Man's coming back. He'll be back here and everything will be fine."

Then Guy was back in Methodist Hospital. The news report of November 2 simply said that Guy was in for treatment "following

Courtesy of Saul Richman

Guy at the 1964 World's Fair in New York City.

recent surgery to repair a weakened major blood vessel." The family worried.

On Saturday, November 7 at 10:45 in the evening Guy Lombardo died. Lilliebell was at his side.

"On this Saturday night," Kenny says, "we were playing in a little town just across the river and outside Manchester, New Hampshire. We had played there many times. We were playing the date and I was standing in front of the band. Now I want something very clear in your book: I was *not* leading the band. The only reason that I was standing up in front of the band is because Lebert couldn't play and announce the numbers at the same time, and he couldn't holler loud enough over the band. So little Joe Van Blurt, the drummer, and I laid out a program exactly the way Guy used to do it and all I was doing in front of the bandstand was making sure that everybody knew what was coming next from the list, calling the tunes, and answering the questions that came from the crowd." Kenny did not sway and move his hands in the way Guy had done. Elaine says, "He didn't profess to take Guy's place."

Kenny continues, "I'm cursed with an ability to see the big picture, some kind of a premonition. Now I realize how this is going to sound, but I was standing there in front of the band and about ten minutes before the job was over I felt a cold breeze come over me and I walked over to Ty Lemley, the singer and guitar player, and I said, 'Lemley, there's something wrong. I don't know what it is, but there's something wrong. We're going to break it up.' Now that never happens in this band. We always go overtime which meant we probably had another fifteen minutes to play. So I gave the signal for the theme and everybody looked at me, but I'm the guy up in front so that's the way you go. We went into the theme 'Auld Lang Syne,' and I said good-bye. We got out and got into the bus. When we got back to the hotel, about half a mile down the road, the clerk had a message from Elaine."

Elaine continues, "My brother Joe had called me. It was just about a quarter to twelve and he said that Guy had died. So right away I called the hotel and spoke to the room clerk and I said, 'Please is Kenny Gardner back?' I didn't know if it was a dance or concert. They play concerts for only two hours. I didn't know that this night it was a dance and I thought for sure Kenny would be at the hotel."

Elaine was extremely close to her eldest brother, Guy, and for her his passing was painful. "I can't believe it yet. You know I was with Carmen three weeks before he died. They had a beautiful condominium in Florida and I stayed with them. I went down twice. We were on the road and Florence, his wife, asked me if I would come in January and Carm was very sick so we flew him back to Houston. When he came back to Florida I stayed with him a couple of weeks and then I joined the band. Then about April they called me again, we were still on the road, and I went down again. We sort of expected his death because Carm was in bed and he wasn't getting any better. We knew he was sick. A nurse from Houston, one of Debakey's top nurses, was there too, and we just knew he couldn't get better. It's different when you sort of expect it. But Guy! Every day we expected him to come back."

Guy's body was flown back to Long Island and put on view from noon until ten on the evening of Monday, November 7 and Tuesday, November 8. Funeral services were held at the Church of the Redeemer in Freeport, Long Island, and interment was at Pinelawn Memorial Park, Pinelawn, Long Island. Mrs. Lombardo asked mourners not to send flowers, but to make donations to Dr. Michael E. Debakey, Baylor School of Medicine, Houston, Texas.

People all over North America showed their grief openly. In London, Ontario, Hubert Lombardo, Guy's first cousin, said that as he prepared for church that Sunday morning the phone rang incessantly as Guy's fans heard the news broadcast over the Canadian Broadcasting Corporation's radio network. The *London Free Press* newspaper, which ran pages of material describing the famous hometown boy, proudly declared, "A CBS official said Sunday the network received more telephoned inquiries about Lombardo's death than it did about those of Elvis Presley earlier this year and Bing Crosby a few weeks ago."

Within a few days, Lebert, the surviving brother of the original three, took the Royal Canadians back out on the road. That was what his brother would have wanted. Playing music and entertaining people had been Guy's life.

It was left to Sam Fink, Guy's lifelong London friend, to put the sense of loss, the long years of Lombardoisms to rest. "When I heard of Guy's death," he said, "I thought of Guy and I felt so sad . . ."

Auld Lang Syne

And for auld syne, my jo,
   For auld lang syne.
We'll tak a cup o' kindness yet,
   For auld land syne.

I

Should auld acquaintance be forgot,
   And never brought to mind?
Should auld acquaintance be forgot,
   And days of auld lang syne?

II

And surely ye'll be your pint stowp!
   And surely I'll be mine!
And we'll tak a cup o' kindness yet,
   For auld lang syne.

III

We twa hae run about the braes
   And pu'd the gowans fine;
But we've wander'd mony a weary foot
   Sin auld lang syne.

IV

We twa hae paidl'd i' the burn
   Frae mornin' sun till dine;
But seas between us braid hae roar'd
   Sin auld lang syne.

V

And there's a hand, my trusty fiere!
   And gie's a hand o' thine!
And we'll take a right guid-willy waught,
   For auld lang syne.

Robert Burns

14 Future Successes

When Guy died in 1977, part of the Royal Canadians died with him. But although Guy, the vocal, visible leader of the orchestra had gone, its core was intact, hard and resilient. The Royal Canadians are as much alive as ever.

Guy's death meant a change in leadership. Lebert was now the sole owner of the band. But Lebert did not want to "front" the orchestra as it was too difficult to play the trumpet and announce songs at the same time. Lebert's brother-in-law, Kenny Gardner, was due to retire. So Victor, who had returned to the orchestra at Guy's request when the bandleader first became ill, became the new orchestra leader.

Victor looked good on stage, bore a great physical resemblance to Guy, and led the Royal Canadians through the emotional New Year's Eve program of 1977. However, there were irreconcilable differences between Lebert and Victor, according to the late Saul Richman, Publicity Manager for the Royal Canadians. Victor left the band.

Within a few months, Bill Lombardo, Lebert's son, became the new orchestra leader and master of ceremonies. Bill was a natural choice. A fine musician in his own right, Bill had played drums with the Royal Canadians a few years before and loved the music. The band would still be one hundred percent Lombardo.

On May 27, 1978, the Royal Canadians were playing at Wonderland in London, Ontario. The music as always was

Bill Lombardo in 1978.

Bill Lombardo conducts the Royal Canadians in 1978.

dreamily smooth, the tone romantic and nostalgic, and Bill, in a black tuxedo, looked right in place swaying to and fro across the stage. The audience loved the youthful bandleader: when he took to the drums to play a solo, all dancing stopped, and the audience cheered him on. The author heard one listener say, "It's not the same without Kenny Gardner," while other immediately replied, "True, but that Bill sure is terrific!"

The late Saul Richman felt the band would continue in its strength under Bill's leadership. "It will be a rough future, but the sweetest music this side of heaven that Guy created is there permanently. There is the Lombardo warmth. There is a discrepancy between the audiences' ages and Bill's, but that is good. Bill has the same rapport, the same enjoyment of the music, the same charisma Guy had. Guy was an old friend to the audiences and now the friends are encouraging Bill, rooting for him. The people *want* the band to continue."

Everyone who knows them is optimistic about the future success of both Bill and the Royal Canadians. "I believe if they pick and choose their engagements they can go on and on and on," says Kenny Gardner.

And Alec Davidson comments enthusiastically when asked about

Lebert Lombardo's son, Bill, now leader of the band, started his musical career early.

Bill. "I like him. Bill is very poised when introducing his father and so on. The songs are newer. The band right now is sparkling!"

After the show, Bill found time to chat with the author about his background and his hopes for the band's future. That conversation is far from being the end of the Lombardo story. It is simply the beginning of the chapters that have yet to be written.

Author: How old are you?

Bill: I'll be thirty-two next April, 1979.

Author: Are you married and do you have children?

Bill: Yes, my wife's name is Diane. We have two children: Adam Tanner who is five and a half years old and Sarah Elizabeth who is a year and a half.

Author: Are they named after any of your aunts and uncles?

Bill: Strangely enough, on my wife's side.

Author: What is your official position with the Royal Canadians?

Bill: I'm orchestra leader and master of ceremonies.

Author: Are you taking the position held by your uncle Guy, basically?

Bill: Yes, I am.

Author: What about your father? What is he going to be doing?

Courtesy of Bill Lombardo

Bill Lombardo leading his own band in California.

Bill: He is still playing trumpet and he is owner of the band. Right now I have something to say, but my father's in charge and he makes the final decisions.

Author: The question naturally follows, why is your father not being the visible leader and conducting the orchestra?

Bill: He likes to play his trumpet and does not want to be a "front" person. He doesn't want to deal with the media and so on.

Author: Are you in charge of positioning the band onstage and saying which number will be played next?

Bill: I do all those things.

Author: What kind of educational and musical background do you have?

Bill: I went to college and received my Associate of Arts degree. As for music, I was in bands all through high school and college. I wasn't trained then, I just started playing. Later I took private instruction from a percussion school in California. I got my experience playing drums in clubs.

Author: You were with the Royal Canadians as a drummer before, weren't you?

Bill: Yes, I was with the band in 1971 and 1972. I left the band the first time to resume my schooling in California and the second time because my wife was having our first baby and I wanted to be with her.

Author: You at one time played rock and roll. Are you completely happy with the Lombardo sound now?

Bill: It's Lombardo style now for me, totally. I want to carry on the band, I don't want to change it. Our New Year's Eve broadcasts will continue and all the old melodies, like the "Piano Medley," "Coquette Medley," and "Harbour Medley," that have been done for years will be the same.

Author: Will you sing or play the drums in the orchestra?

Bill: We have a fine vocalist right now. Although I am above all trying to establish my identity as the leader, one of my great loves is singing and I hope to be doing more vocals as time goes on. I'm singing in the trio on songs like "Boo Hoo" and I play drums on the song "South Rampart Street Parade."

Author: On my ticket it says Guy Lombardo's Royal Canadians. Do you propose to continue using this name?

Bill: Yes, it does say Guy Lombardo's Royal Canadians which is proper, is correct: It's Guy Lombardo's Royal Canadians with or without him!

Even Guy's name was perfect for the band, it's so catchy. What a guy! What a great guy! I want to keep this band going to a great future.

Author: How many months a year does the band tour now?

Bill: Oh, pretty much ten months.

Author: Is that going to continue or will the band be looking for a sit-down job?

Bill: Those days are pretty well gone now. That's what my father would say if he was sitting here now. I want to keep the band working and bringing the music to the people as the Lombardo band has always done. But I wouldn't mind a sit-down job for part of the year.

Author: Do you find touring this much hard in terms of your private life?

Bill: It is sacrificing time together for we are a close family, but my wife understands I have a future in this orchestra. She wants me to be happy.

Author: I'll bet your father is really happy to have you back in the orchestra.

Bill: Yes, and I'm extremely happy to be here. You know it's like a candle that's burning and has reached a certain point. It's all new and it's so gratifying. Dad and I went to see my Great Aunt Josie Lombardo—Great Uncle Frank's wife—today here in London. This family is such a fantastic miracle. I asked her what possessed my family to end up on the little itty bitty island Lipari? And why did they land in London? And to hear her talk about Lipari! I think of my son and daughter and the feeling parents have about children and it gave me a completed kind of feeling.

Dad and I went "buddying" around town today and he showed me where they lived and where they played their early jobs. We saw his school and Adam Beck's place. I know the two of us being together meant a lot to him and it meant a lot to me too. We enjoy coming to London.

We Lombardos are really proud of our family, we are family-oriented, and stick together. It's a great thrill when you're blessed to live long enough to see your children grow up!

Author: Do you think your father will retire and leave the band soon?

Bill: It's hard to say. He deserves it.

Author: In summation?

Bill: I want to keep the band working. What I have basically is a fantastic name that is gold all over the world. I want to keep the band on top.

Bill Lombardo

Courtesy of Sue Fink

All of the following songs were written by Carmen Lombardo. In many cases, the songs were a joint effort by Lombardo and his music-writing partner, John Jacob Loeb.

This list has been complied by Mr. Dave Kressley of New Tripoli, Pennsylvania and Mr. Dick Scher of Chicago, Illinois and is reproduced here with Mr. Kressley's kind permission.

Mr. Kressley is perhaps the Royal Canadians' greatest fan. His collection of Lombardo items includes five hundred and seventy-six singles, one hundred and fourteen albums, four hundred song sheets, and six hundred tapes of radio and television shows in which the band appeared.

Title and Date	Co-Writer(s)
Address Unknown (1939)	Dedette Lee Hill; Johnny Marks
Affection (1931)	Jimmy Monaco; Al Bryan
After Thinking It Over (1929)	Benny Davis
After Tonight (1932)	Cliff Friend
Alabama Beauty Shop (1935)	Joe Young; Fred E. Ahlert
Aloha, Nui, Loa (1947)	Chester Conn
As Long as Love Lives On (1932)	Joe Young
Awakening (1935)	Tot Seymour; Vee Lawnhurst
Back Home for Keeps (1945)	Bob Russell
Bath Parade, The (from *Arabian Nights*) (1954)	John Jacob Loeb
Beautiful Lady (1934)	Cliff Friend
Bells of Portofino (1962)	John Jacob Loeb
Between the Pages (1932)	Harry Pease
Beyond the Clouds	John Jacob Loeb
Blue Nile (1935)	C. L. used the name "Joe London"; Cliff Friend; Charlie Tobias

Blue Willows (1953)	Buddy Kaye
Boo-Hoo (1937)	Edward Heyman; John Jacob Loeb
Broken Hearted (1926)	Al Lewis; Richard A. Whiting
Can't You See I'm Lonely? (new version) (1930)	Gus Kahn (Original by Felix F. Feist and Harry Armstrong)
Carmencita (The Lombardo Tango) (1934)	George Clarke; Bert Clarke
Cocoanut Wireless (from *Paradise Island*) (1961)	John Jacob Loeb
Come Along Down (from *Mardi Gras*)	John Jacob Loeb
Confucius Say (1939)	Cliff Friend
Congratulations to You (1952)	Sunny Clapp
Coquette (1928)	Gus Kahn; John W. Green
Crossword Puzzle Crazy (c. 1925)	C. L. probably wrote this alone
Cy (1924)	Fred Kreitzer
Dance with Me (1934)	Sam Coslow
Don't Let the Parade Pass You By (1932)	Joe Young
Don't Wait Until the Lights Are Low	Howard Johnson
Down with Whiskey (from *Mardi Gras*)	John Jacob Loeb
Dream Places (Introduction: Please Let Me Dream in Your Arms) (1929)	Al Lewis; Al Sherman
Dream Stars (1934)	Cliff Friend
Dreamy Eyes (1937)	John Jacob Loeb
Every Night's Like New Year's Eve (1949)	Sam Stept
Ferdinand the Bull (Not the well-known song with the same title) (1938)	John Jacob Loeb
Footloose and Fancy-Free (1935)	Gus Kahn
For Old Times' Sake (1932)	Gus Kahn
Freckle Face, You're Beautiful (1934)	Cliff Friend
Gazing at a Blazing Fire (1936)	Charlie Tobias; Henry Tobias
Get Out Those Old Records (1950)	John Jacob Loeb
Give Me Your Affection, Honey (1931)	Al Bryan; Pete Wendling
Good Night, Good Luck and God Bless You (1954)	Composed by C. L. as a sign-off tune in a 1954 filmed TV show
Good Night My Lady Love (1932)	Joe Young
Goose Hangs High, The (1936)	Cliff Friend
Grand Vizier's Lament, The (from *Arabian Nights*) (1954)	John Jacob Loeb
Hail to the Sultan (from *Arabian Nights*) (1954)	John Jacob Loeb
Hand in Hand (1928)	Harry Harris; possibly Barris
Happy New Year, Darling (1946)	Johnny Marks
Heaven Help Me (1934)	Milton Drake; Walter Kent
Hero of All My Dreams, The (from *Arabian Nights*) (1954)	John Jacob Loeb
He, She and Me (1929)	Charles Newman
Hilltop Heaven (1931)	Edward Eliscu
Honky Tonk Sweetheart (1952)	Sunny Clapp

How Long Has It Been? (from *Arabian Nights*) (1954) — John Jacob Loeb
Hula Rhumba, The (1952) — John Jacob Loeb
I'd Know That Smile (from *Mardi Gras*) — John Jacob Loeb
I Fell Asleep with Your Name on My Lips (1928) — Al Sherman; Al Lewis
I Love to Bumpity Bump (On a Bumpy Road with You) (1928) — Al Sherman; Al Lewis
I Love You with All My Heart (1938) — John Jacob Loeb
I Ought to Have My Head Examined — John Jacob Loeb
I'm Glad You Met Me (1931) — Edward Heyman
Imitation of Love (1935) — Dave Dreyer; Gordon Clifford
I'm King Again (1935) — Cliff Friend
In a Dream (1930) — Fred Higman
In a Little Carolina Town (1937) — John Jacob Loeb
In My Estimation of You (1936) — Benny Davis; J. Fred Coots
In Our Little Helicopter (1943) — John Jacob Loeb
In the Neighborhood of Heaven (1938) — John Jacob Loeb
It Must Have Been Two Other People (1939) — J. Lawrence; A. Altman
It's a Small World After All (1936) — John Jacob Loeb
It's Easier Said Than Done (1937) — John Jacob Loeb
It's Great to Be Alive (from *Arabian Nights*) (1954) — John Jacob Loeb
It's Never Too Late (1939) — John Jacob Loeb
I've Got My Eye on You — Milton Drake; Walter Kent
Jungle Drums (Canto Karabali) (American version) (c. 1933) — Charles O'Flynn (Original Ernesto Lecuona)
Kind of a Girl (from *Mardi Gras*) — John Jacob Loeb
Kissable Baby (1931) — Dave Dreyer; Lu C. Bender
Ladies of the Ballet (from *Mardi Gras*) — John Jacob Loeb
Lane in Spain, A (1926) — Al Lewis
Last Night I Dreamed You Kissed Me (1928) — Gus Kahn
Let Me Hear Our Love Song — Herb Magidson; Sam Stept
Let's Give Love Another Chance (1931) — Herb Magidson; Sam Stept
Let's Tee Off Together (1936) — John Jacob Loeb; Charlie Tobias
Lights Are Low, The (The Music Is Sweet) (1934) — Cliff Friend
Liliuokalani (c. 1949) — Arnold Johnson
Little Fairy Waltz, The (1951) — Larry Stock
Little Love Will Go a Long, Long Way, A (1938) — John Jacob Loeb
Little Shepherd of My Dreams (1939) — Stanley Adams
Long Ago Love, A (from *Arabian Nights*) (1954) — John Jacob Loeb
Love Marches On (1936) — Charlie Tobias
Lovers Lane Is Lonesome Lane for Me (1929) — Charles Newman; Nelson Chon

Love Was Born	Gladys Shelley
Maid in Havana (The Lombardo Rhumba) (1934)	George Clarke; Bert Clarke
Ma, I Miss Your Apple Pie (1941)	John Jacob Loeb
Makin' Time with You (1930)	Tot Seymour
Marchin' Towards Ya', Georgia (1934)	Cliff Friend
Mardi Gras Waltz, The (from *Mardi Gras*)	John Jacob Loeb
Marry the One You Love (from *Arabian Nights*) (1954)	John Jacob Loeb
Maybe (1937)	John Jacob Loeb; Kogen
Mist on the Moon (1950)	Johnny Marks
Moment in the Dark, A (1932)	Arthur Freed
Moonlight March, The	Charles Newman
Mumbo Jumbo (from *Mardi Gras*)	John Jacob Loeb
My Day (1937)	John Jacob Loeb; Ed Heyman
My Heart's in the Right Place (1934)	James V. Monaco; Charles Newman
My Room	
My Sentimental Heart (1952)	John Jacob Loeb
My Sugar Takes Me with a Grain of Salt (1936)	John Jacob Loeb
My Victory (Was Conquering Your Heart) (1929)	Ned Miller; Jules K. Stein
In My World and Your World (from *Paradise Island*) (c. 1961)	John Jacob Loeb
Napoli (1959)	Danny DiMinno
Next to Your Mother, Who Do You Love? (1931)	Joe Young
Night on the Water, (There Was A) (1933)	George Clarke; Bert Clarke; Ellery Rand
No More Love ('Cause There Is No More You) (1932)	Cliff Friend
No One Could Love You, As Much As I Do (1932)	Joe Young
Nothing but the Best (1933)	Charles Tobias; Gerald Marks
Oahu (My Lovely Island Home) (1947)	Carmen wrote words and music
Oh! Moytle (1945)	Charles Tobias
Old New England Moon (c. 1936)	Charles Tobias; John Jacob Loeb
Oooh! I Wanna Have a Little Dance with You (1936)	Joe Young; Fred E. Ahlert
Oooh! Look-A-There, Ain't She Pretty? (1933)	Clarence Todd
Our Little Ranch House (1950)	John Jacob Loeb
Out of My Dreams, into My Arms (1929)	Nat Conney
Paradise Island (from *Paradise Island*) (1961)	John Jacob Loeb
Pardon	Danny DiMinno
Pirate's Lament, A (from *Mardi Gras*)	John Jacob Loeb
Pirate's Polka (from *Mardi Gras*)	John Jacob Loeb
Play Ball with the N.Y. Mets (1962)	Tom McDonald

Pleasant Dreams (1932) — Sam Coslow

Please Bring My Daddy a Train, Santa
(1953) — John Jacob Loeb

Please Let Me Dream in Your Arms (1928) — Al Sherman; Al Lewis

Poor People (1928) — Art Kassel

Powder Your Face with Sunshine (Smile!
Smile! Smile!) (1948) — Stanley Rochinski

Return to Me (Ritornaa Me) (1957) — Danny DiMinno

Ridin' Around in the Rain (1934) — Gene Austin

Rollin' Stone (1939) — John Jacob Loeb

Rosette (1928) — Charles Newman

'Round My Heart (1932) — Joe Young

Sailboat in the Moonlight, A (1937) — John Jacob Loeb

Say "Hello" to the Folks Back Home (1930) — Benny Davis

Seems Like Old Times (1945) — John Jacob Loeb

Sharing (My Love with You) (1932) — Joe Young; Sam Stept

She Will Be Standing in the Harbor (1943) — John Jacob Loeb

Silver Threads and Golden Dreams

Since He Traded His Zoot Suit for a Uniform
(1942) — Pat Innisfree

Snuggled on Your Shoulder (1932) — Joe Young

Someone I Could Love (from *Mardi Gras*) — John Jacob Loeb

Some Rainy Day (1939) — John Jacob Loeb

Sometimes (1941) — Gus Kahn

Springtime Is Here Again (1951) — John Jacob Loeb

Sunshowers (1952) — John Jacob Loeb

Sun Valley Rose (1942) — Johnny Franks; Eddie Lyon

Sweet Che-waukla, The Land of Sleepy
Water (1929) — Fred C. Higman

Sweet Dreams (1927) — Richard A. Whiting; Seymour Simons

Sweetest Little Honey (1928) — Marty Bloom; Art Kassel

Sweetest Music This Side of Heaven, The
(used in the film *Many Happy Returns*)
(1934) — Cliff Friend

Sweethearts on Parade (1928) — Charles Newman

Sweetheart Waltz, The (1934) — Milton Drake; Walter Kent

Sweetness (1929) — Ned Miller; Chester Cohn

Takes You (1929) — Benny Davis

Teenie Weenie Genie (from *Arabian Nights*)
(1954) — John Jacob Loeb

Tell Me Little Daisy (1927) — Jack L. Miles

That's All I'll Ever Ask of You (1951) — John Jacob Loeb

That's Something to Be Thankful For (1932) — Joe Young

Then I Could Forget You (1936) — Lebert Lombardo; Cliff Friend

There Goes My Dream (1954) — Sunny Clapp

There'll Never Be Another Waltz Like This
(The Lombardo Waltz) (1934) — Paul Hill, Al Lewis

There's a Shadow in the Sunshine of Your Smile (1935)	Joe Young; Fred E. Ahlert
There's Romance in the Air (1932)	Joe Young; George W. Meyer
There's Something in Your Eyes (American version) (1932)	Eng. version: Reg Connelly; music by Franz Grothe
There Will Always Be Someone to Turn To (1958)	Danny DiMinno
There Won't Be a Shortage of Love (1942)	John Jacob Loeb
They Satisfy (1930)	Gus Kahn
Thousand and One Nights, A (from *Arabian Nights*) (1954)	John Jacob Loeb
Thrill of a Lifetime, The (used in the 1938 Paramount film *The Thrill of A Lifetime*) (1938)	Hollander; Sam Coslow
Thrill, The (1934)	Dave Franklin
Tierra-Verde (c. 1963) (Used as the theme song by Guy Lombardo on some of his radio and TV shows from the Port-O-Call Restaurant in Tierra-Verde, Fla.)	
Tiny Old Town (1940)	Stanley Adams
Token of Love (1930)	Sam Coslow; Larry Spier
Tom-Boy (1931)	Joe Young; Larry Owen
Toodle-oo (1937)	John Jacob Loeb
Until We Meet Again Sweetheart (1930)	Harry Link; Dorothy Dick
Waiting (1928)	I. J. Faggen
Wake Up and Sing (1936)	Cliff Friend; Charlie Tobias
Waltz I Can't Forget, The (1928)	Gus Kahn
Waltz That Brought You Back to Me, The (1932)	Irving Caesar
Waltzing in the Carolines (1933)	Joe Young
Was It You? (1931)	Jack Scholl; Dave Dreyer
We'll See It Through (1932)	Cliff Friend
We're Getting Closer to Love (1933)	Dave Oppenheim; Ira Schuster
Whale of a Story, A (from *Arabian Nights*) (1954)	John Jacob Loeb
What an Existence (1932)	Joe Young
What a Night (used in the 1934 Fox film *Bachelor of Arts*) (1934)	Cliff Friend
What a Pity (from *Arabian Nights*) (1954)	John Jacob Loeb
What Have We Done to Our World? (1971)	(Carmen's last song)
What've You Got to Lose But Your Heart?	
When I Take My Lady (from *Mardi Gras*)	John Jacob Loeb
When My Man Sails Home (from *Mardi Gras*)	John Jacob Loeb
Where Are You Gonna Be When the Moon Shines? (1950)	John Jacob Loeb

Where in the World Is There Someone for
Me?
Whisper That You Love Me (1932)   Roy Turk
Whistle and Blow Your Blues Away (1932)   Joe Young
Who Loves You, I Do (1931)   Bennee Russel

Why Did It Have to Be Me? (You Knew
You'd Hurt Somebody) (1931)   Bud Green; Sam Stept
Why Did You? (You Made Me Love You)
(1929)   Mickey Kippel
Why Should We Both Be Lonely? (from *Ara-*
bian Nights) (1954)   John Jacob Loeb
With a Smile on My Face (And a Tear in My
Heart) (1930)   Dave Oppenheim; Al Piantadosi
You Are the Girl I Can't Forget (1930)
You Belong to Me, I Belong to You (1929)   Charles Newman
You Better Play Ball with Me (1936)   Charles Tobias; John Jacob Loeb
You Lead the Parade (1934)   Milton Drake; Walter Kent
You'll Know When It Happens (1946)   John Jacob Loeb
You're Beautiful Tonight, My Dear (1933)
(Recorded by Bing Crosby & Guy Lombardo
Orchestra on 1/31/33.)   Joe Young
You're Everything Beautiful (1936)   Benny Davis; J. Fred Coots
You're Gonna Be Surprised Tonight (1933)   Mort Dixon
You're the Sweetest Girl This Side of Heaven
(1930)   Gus Kahn; Harry Archer
Yours with Love and Kisses (1947)

The following songs were written by Guy Lombardo in conjunction with other writers.

This list has been compiled by Mr. Dave Kressley and Mr. Dick Scher and is reproduced here with Mr. Kressley's kind permission.

Title and Date	Co-writer(s)
If You're Thinking of Me (1929)	Julian Davidson; Art Sizemore
Joe College (1929)	J. Paul Fogarty; Ted Fiorito
Little Stranger (1929)	Jimmy Steiger
Rag-Time Musketeers (1930)	Billy Frisch; Otto Motzan
Sunbonnet Days (1929)	Bernie Grossman; Clinton Keithley
Wooing (1930)	Ned Miller; Chauncey Haines, Jr.
Take a Chance with Me (And I'll Take a Chance with You) (1927)	Al Lewis; Harold A. Dellon
That's All I Ask of You (1929)	Mickey Kippel

A Basic Discography of Lombardo Albums Available Today
The following information was compiled by the author.

Drifting and Dreaming	Capitol	SM-1593
Is That All There Is?	Capitol	SM-340
Your Guy Lombardo Medley	Capitol	SM-739
Best of Guy Lombardo Vol. 1	MCA	MCA2-4041
Best of Guy Lombardo Vol. 2	MCA	MCA2-4082
Dance in the Moonlight	MCA	VL 73605
Dance Medley Time	MCA	MCA 242
Golden Medleys	MCA	MCA 103
Greatest Hits	MCA	MCA 245
Here's Guy Lombardo	MCA	VL 73833
Song in My Heart	MCA	CB 20032
Legendary Performer	RCA	CPL 12047
The Best of Guy Lombardo 6 volumes	Reader's Digest	2729

Index